Internal Pieces
By
LaMont E. Walker

Internal Pieces

For Booking & Contact Information:
cecopublishing@gmail.com

All scripture references are from the King James Version of the Holy Bible, unless otherwise noted.

Poems with asterisks denote hymnal references.

Poems by third parties were used with their permission.

Cover Design by LaToya Stevens

ISBN: 978-0-9836336-2-4

CECO Publishing
Est. 2011

Book Dedication

This book is dedicated to all of those whose hearts has been broken by what you could not have and to those who have transformed their pain into power for living. First and definitely last, to Jesus Christ who gave me new life filled with exciting adventures of love, peace, and victory.

I love you,

Mont**

Table of Contents

Introduction

Pieces of me, pieces of relationship, love pieces, creative pieces and pieces of spirituality are some the internal pieces of me. All of these are inspired by real and true events, but some are laced with a touch of imagination.

Pieces of Me

Within this section, you will find many thoughts, most of which are just now being made privy to you and the entire world. Most artists from singers, to dancers, and even painters, never verbalize their thoughts. They use the art to express the thought and emotion. Prepare yourself for this rollercoaster ride of emotions!

This Day That the Lord Has Made

By: LaMont Walker

This day that the Lord has made,

How can I rejoice when there's no aid?

This day that the Lord has made.

This day that the Lord has made

It seems as if the madness will never end.

Love, anger, happiness, frustration

All saying come around this bend

This day that the Lord has made

This day that the Lord has made

Why did He make this one at all

My back is hurting from all of the bites

By the people who are supposed to be Israelites

This day that the Lord has made

This day that the Lord has made

Filled with gloom from all the sadness in the room

A friend, a brother, a relative, my uncle

Passed away oh so soon.

This day that the Lord has made

This day that the Lord has made

I really enjoyed this one and hoped it'd never end

Because this was the day I found the truest Friend

He said He'd never leave me

This day that the Lord has made

This day that the Lord has made

My Friend was still there and said,

Rest today, all your burdens I'll bear

This day that the Lord has made

This day that the Lord has made,

I thought I was out of my mind

10 years of crying, pain, suffering, agony!

And my Friend bore it all

This day that the Lord has made.

This day that the Lord has made,

Has made me realize that I could never be separated

From my Friend's love

Solid as a boulder, pure snow white as a dove,

This day that the Lord has made.

Colors

By: LaMont Walker

Blue.

I woke up this morning and the sky was blue.

Before I could even have breakfast, it was black.

Black.

I failed the test, even though I'd done my best.

This time I was laid to rest, as my eyes cried until red.

Red.

I'm full of energy and know that I can handle whatever.

Then it comes and hits me, a light that shines as bright as white.

White.

I'm pure, I'm free, no more chains are holding me.

As I ease on down the road, I see gold.

Gold.

I'm not rich so why even front?

Because nobody wants me to be blunt like lime.

Lime.

I am spontaneous, frisky, and risky,

But hold up because I ain't misty like grey.

Grey.

I will not be dull, dry and bored. Just think,

What would it feel like if I were pink?

Pink.

Not many people like me because I'm real.

I'm in your face and you can't ignore me like teal.

Teal.

I'll go with the flow today and maybe tomorrow.

It depends if I get a visit from an old friend Mr. Brown Sorrow.

Brown.

I am earth, I am dirt, I am man.

Yes even the Man with the Master plan.

I could go on forever and ever you see,

But that's just the key!

You must have vision to see!

To see the many colors that are inside of me!

A rainbow. Yes a rainbow deep within!

Follow it to the end and you won't find gold,

But you'll find a priceless story that's never been told.

Why I Walk in The Rain?

By: Lyrikal Virtuoso

You gaze in awe as you pass me by/Laughing, pointing and wondering why the hell I'm even out in this rain/I continue walking straightforward to no destination while lightening strikes and the sun goes to sleep/Something about the night causes all of the day's problems, concerns and doubts to surface/This time that should be dedicated to rest, is typically spent in stress/Those feelings you try so hard to look past and blow off succumb you the second you attempt to close your eyes/Perhaps the darkness of the night is synonymous to the darkness you see when your eyes are shut/The faces of those that hurt you appear with every blink and sleep may never come/What's next?/Well, I like to take walks so no one can see me thinking/Listen to music so that joyful words can replace the hurtful ones that you instilled in my heart/Read a book in hopes of replacing one of its chapters with a chapter in my life/Write poems from my heart with high hopes of transferring my pain to paper/Pride keeps a smile on my face even when inside I die slowly/Prayer keeps me hoping for something better in life but there's something about the rain that falls during life's storms that keep me grounded/Cleansing the earth and providing growth is its purpose to fulfill/Every new day has soiled me with hurt, pain, confusion and anger/So why did I walk in the rain you ask?/Crying cleanses the soul and the rain conceals my tears

The Forms of Alone

By: LaMont Walker

As I sat alone today
I began to stir the thoughts of my mind's curd and whey.
I sat there thinking why am I ahead of my time?
No one to connect with, and the one I want to be with is viewed as a crime.
These are only the beginning of the thoughts I feel deep down in my bone,
As I sat there in my chair, being all alone.

I wanted to go to sleep, but then the thoughts are magnified.
Some times all I want to do is dream,
But from the images I see, all I can do is scream.
Ain't gonna sleep no more, no more, I groan
While I lay there in my bed, being all alone.

You tried loving me, but you didn't know what it would take.
Long midnight conversations, not really saying anything, just keeping me awake.
I loved it because you kept me from sleeping,
But I knew it would all end one day and then I found myself weeping.
Weeping because I wanted you and you wanted me,
But knowing the truth of reality, we could never escape our family.
I waved goodbye to you in the airport as if in the twilight zone,
And there I stood again, being all alone.

Now, not only do I sit, lie, and stand alone,
But I live in the comfort of my home all alone.
Within those four walls I sing and I dance in a very loud tone
About all of the happiness and joy I never knew from being all alone.

Alone is a position that you choose to be in
Especially after you've been hurt by a so-called friend.
Alone is a medicine that you take

When you've become diseased by all of the people who are fake.

Alone is a place in your mind

Where everything and everyone is kind.

I told a friend that it's okay to be alone,

Because being alone allows you the time to become more unique.

It gives you the time to enhance your physique and that makes you more attractive.

Who doesn't want to be more attractive?

If you say I don't, I would say you're a liar

And test you to see if you would burn all of your expensive clothes & jewelry in the fire.

I spoke to Mr. Alone today

And told him I wouldn't need him to come my way.

I met and talked to Ms. Joy over the phone,

And we determined that we didn't need to be alone.

At least for now.

With Me

By: LaMont Walker

This is the last day and I'm feeling it with no senses,
People with pre-conceived notions always misses, with me.
I'll be strolling down the harbor viewing the crystal clear sea,
And I'll have my two happy brothers along with me.

With me, there is no end of my life's story,
I've had so many tests and trials, but I give God all the glory.
I give Him the glory because He's the one that taught me,
Brought me, and trained me on how to keep my sanity.

With me, I love to gaze at bright colors, red mostly,
Because it helps me to keep my life full of vitality!
Energy, power, fuel to burn,
I said my favorite color is red and from that I'll never turn.

With me, I'm as sexy, attractive, and as kind as you'll let me be,
Please be careful boo because I'm not going home to meet your family.
Baby don't dis me cause this is the way that I've been built,
A patch of love here, a patch of humor there like your grandma's favorite quilt.

With me, singing is not my job, but my passion,
And only like Christ have I tried to fashion.
I listen Daryl, Carl, Smokie, Marvin and Wanya,
But there is only one true original and that's my boy Tonex.

With me, I'm simple at times, but love complexity.
It keeps some people from getting next to me.
People can be mean, rude heartless and cruel,
But I listen to my God so I won't end up like a fool.

With me, I want to be married with five kids,

If I were to put that up at an auction I would get no bids.

I love my mom, dad, brothers, sister and everybody in the family,

This encompasses God's plan that He initiated back in eternity.

With me, you got to love the Father, Son, & Holy Ghost better known as the Trinity,

Or you and me will never ever walk in true harmony.

Yeah I'll talk to you on a one on one level,

But I will be very watchful because I know my enemy the devil.

All right, alright, I'm very grateful that you've spent this time in my company,

And I hope you have a better understanding about getting with me.

Holding Back

By: LaMont Walker

In the depth of my innermost emotion,

External influences are stirring up commotion.

This stirred up emotion I must keep locked in a sack

Because for you I care so much, I hold back.

I hold back not the emotion,

But words that would cause an explosion.

Yes you would explode with anger, tears, and frustration

As I chose your heart to write my next book of damnation.

You make me sick to my stomach

And instead of losing my cool, these rhymes I kick.

I kick, I spit, I compose and I communicate

My thoughts, my feelings, and my being you can only imitate.

Often times I speak with authority,

With you I hold back because of your sensitivity.

You can't handle me for real.

If you could, you would be as strong as me.

I'm holding back even now on this paper

Because I could speak and make you vanish like vapor

Eventually my mind, heart and soul will release me

And the act of holding back will only be an impossibility.

Invisible Me

By: LaMont Walker

Although you can see me
With your small brown eyes,
You talk and explain without clarity
And I ask if you can see me
But you'll tell me lies.

You will lie because you cannot see the invisible.
I have translated myself while in your presence.
Thoughts of pleasure, joy and uncertainty
Have given me the ability to go unseen.

Everyone has the power to become invisible,
But few know how to tap into it.
This ability comes from every experience
Be it love, hate, senses, and conversations that are intense.

In this invisible world where I am
You can test yourself and never have to cram.
Test yourself on what you might ask,
Test your feelings for the one who sees only the visible.

This Morning

By: LaMont Walker

Waking up this morning
Feeling like mourning
Because of the reality of my life
Seems to be filled with so much strife.
Loneliness prepared my breakfast
With hurt and anger as the main sources of protein and minerals.
A glass of secrets was cold and waiting to be swallowed,
But the truth of it all I decided to follow.

As I view through the eyes of verity,
It is there that I understand the severity;
The graveness of rising with a new daybreak
Causes my destiny to be what I make.
What I make, what I create, what I exhilarate,
Is determined by the attitude
Which will regulate the altitude.

Should I choose to mourn?
It will be over the glass of secrets spilled;
But that which is spilled can definitely be dried.
I refuse the protein and minerals and keep my pride,
Not to the extent of being foolish
Because wisdom has taught me better than that.

The mourning has passed
And the day grows brighter.
Strengthen your legs and arms to become a fighter
Because this morning belongs to you.

I Reminisced

By: LaMont Walker

The thoughts of my mind deepened
As I reviewed the attacks of 9/11
Many souls and hearts perished,
And I prayed they made it to heaven.

I continued reflecting on the events
That devastated our impenetrable country,
It was an act that Americans will never forget.
We thought we'd see it only in movies and not the 21st century.

My mouth dropped.
My heart sank.
My stomach turned sour
And it all happened within an hour.
One tower was hit and then another,
But no one expected a tragedy any further.
The twin tower was hit and it swayed
And many Americans watched while being dismayed.

It seemed as if the tears would never end
Because too many people lost a friend.
Coffee breaks will be silent.
Lunch will never be the same.
Our hope and desire is that we can breathe again.
Our eyes open filled with the sun.
Our smiles return again loaded with happiness.
We will always remember and never forget
Everything we lost and gained in the unseen atrocity we met.

Are You Listening?

By: LaMont Walker

Thoughts of you make me scream!

I wish and hope that this is a dream!

I want you so bad

But do you want me to the extreme of mad?

Why do I want to touch your face and feel your skin?

Why do I want to hear you voice again?

When I'm with you I can't concentrate.

Your voice, your laugh, I mentally imitate.

I see you coming and my heart is filled with excitement!

I enjoy being with you

Because I step inside of a place that I long to be!

Why won't you come to me?

Why won't you let me in?

Look at me!

Let your lips speak of me!

Take the palm of your hand

And rub it across my land!

You'll feel the warmth of my white sands.

You'll experience my refreshing waters

That are able to quench every thirst!

Try me and your feelings of loneliness, discomfort, and sadness

I'll burst!

Too Many Days

By: LaMont Walker

Too many days I don't understand
Why this character, item, problem seems unbeatable.
When I wake up, it's there.
As I go to lunch with friends, he shows up.
When I lay my body down, it lies with me.

I wonder, I ponder, and I contemplate,
Will I, won't I, mess with or alter fate.
Sometimes this conglomeration of something is strong
And few days is it weak.
Constantly, consistently, and insistently
Is this person, place or thing.

Why do you taunt me for the rest of my life?
Don't or can't you understand that you're not my wife?
Yes I feel deeply for you in my heart,
But your harm for me is like a bulls-eye to a dart.
Attractive to my senses you truly are,
But you're ill-willed actions to me have gone too far.

Too many days I don't understand,
Why this character, item, and problem is me.

What?

By: LaMont Walker

With you to be I long
The time is wrong tells me my heart.
That not only, but
The prime of my life in am I.

Beautiful times see I with my eyes.
Are you like a rose delicate
For me shines red your pedals
Looking because am I.
True happiness seeks I is what.
In God know I it's found.

Curious Questions

By: LaMont Walker

Have you ever found someone,
Someone with whom you'd love to be one?
Have you ever been afraid to love,
Because past experiences has shattered your heart?
Oh, how you adore the beauty of this angel,
But you're too nervous to speak your core.

How many tears are shared
Because the future isn't promising?
How much stress can your emotion hold
Before they all begin to fold?
Yes, you want to succeed by far,
But unseen forces have crossed the bar.

My search possibly has ended,
But a hasty tongue is not well-blended.
The hurts are now gone
And my love is ready to move on.
Speak you heavenly being filled with light.
Pour into my soul and nourish my sight.

The right now challenges waters the eyes,
But the joy and laughter to come surely dries.
Fold if you must, but don't break or bust.
The truth of emotion survives only by determination.
Denial, fear and pain must go by extermination.
Search until you find your rib and restore it.
Cry until your strength is intensified
But never stop picking your intellect

With curious questions as you recollect.

If I Weren't Here

By: LaMont Walker

Too many times do I want to leave.
Another life, body, and new wife I'll cleave.
Leave this place where I have many memories
And start again where everything is new.

My heart desires to see a friend that hurt.
Maybe if I weren't here, he wouldn't know my dirt.
The closest I'll get to him at this point,
Is by wearing what he left, around my neck;
While talking to another friend, I almost had a wreck.
None of this may have happened,
If I weren't here.

The Son Shine

By: LaMont Walker

Waking up was easy today
My body was yearning for another way.
Another way to start the day;
Get back in bed, wrap under the comforter
And cry myself to sleep hoping for change.

I was on the straight and narrow
Until I gave a much wanted vibe.
I didn't purposely give it,
I just happened to be in the right place,
At the wrong time with the right and wrong person.

Facing the dark knight,
I now find myself giving
To him what used to belong to me;
The joy of my consecration.
He happily took it and rode off laughing,
Leaving me empty until the Son shined.

The Son made me smile again.
The Son gave me back what I lost.
The Son kept me close and breathed into me.

As it turns out,
I am able to live
Because the Son lives in me.
Here's to the Son shine.

Sometimes

By: LaMont Walker

Sometimes.

Sometimes I feel alone.

Sometimes I think you don't care.

Sometimes my heart is heavy.

Sometimes I thought you loved me.

Sometimes I regret giving it up.

Sometimes I wish I hadn't opened my mouth.

Sometimes I want to leave.

Sometimes I don't know where to go.

Sometimes I desire to be in the Prophet's House.

Sometimes I'd like to hide in Empowerment.

Sometimes the inner man cries.

Sometimes I always tell lies.

Sometimes I don't want to hurt.

Sometimes I want to be in love.

Sometimes my arms want to wrap around you.

Sometimes I get excited when you're around.

Sometimes you're all I can think about.

Sometimes I always want to express my secret feelings.

Sometimes nobody will know me.

Sometimes somebody will read me.

Sometimes you'll understand the tears.

Sometimes.

From Death to Life

By: LaMont Walker

Too much pain to deny,
That tonight I want to cry.
Always trying to include everyone,
While being excluded by the ones I love.

During the night of giving thanks
I received many stares filled with blanks.
As I entered the door,
Everyone went into an uproar,
While the older half of me,
Found an exit to flee.
To flee from my presence,
Bur forgetting that I'm his very essence.
So I laughed, I sighed,
But on the inside I cried.

The more I think,
The closer the brink.
Disaster waiting to dance,
If, and only if I give it a chance.
The best of me will not fall,
Because of the strength and trust
I've learned through it all.
I will not die
But I shall live high.
High, not from weed,
Bur from the word of life I feed.

Who is He Talking To?

By: LaMont Walker

Stop disappointing me.
I really want to heal.
Each time the balm I feel,
Another wound is inflicted.

Stop disappointing me.
My eyes would like to see
What does the world or life for that matter
Look like without tears being the lens.

Quit being so far away.
You moved closer, but didn't want to stay.
Some pieces of the ship remained intact;
I've been trying to decipher whether it's relation or friend.

Quit ignoring me to yourself
You see me every time you rise
And when you hold your rose
You look at the frame with my prints.

Block the anger that is secretly speaking.
Easy it would be to allow bitterness to grow.

Suspend all of the negativity
And release all of the creativity.

Discontinue being the last one
And start being the first one.

Love, forgive, and live.

By: LaMont Walker

I surely didn't see today's events
When I awoke from irregular sleep.
After two finals and a pizza, I made a tent.
Into this tent I decided to leap,
Not realizing that I would not be content.

The excitement of closing a chapter
And opening a new one
Continues to drive me from here to ever-after
Happily it might be, once I have my first son.

Back in a hole created for me
I thought I was out and considered myself free.
Only to find out that I wasn't free,
I just moved to another spot
Where deception smiled at me.

I don't like this place
Where I feel trapped
I hope, I pray,
I stay away from being slapped
By another illusion that brings bitterness and confusion.

The Recalling The Revelation
By: LaMont Walker

Sitting across from wisdom
As I recall it,
Many old, but new sensations arose
As I recalled it.
I offered one and allowed another to be touched
As I recall it,
Not realizing the epiphany I was about to experience
As I recalled it.
The more I offered and allowed
As I recall it,
The clearer I could hear the sound
As I recalled it.

What you feel, is what I feel.
I've felt this from the beginning.
You're just coming into the knowledge.
Now you can truly understand
Why the strategy of freedom was implemented.

Once I heard that, I told wisdom to wait
As I recall it,
Because my body, spirit, and soul had been transformed
As I recalled it.

Internal Pieces of 'The Recalling The Revelation':

This particular piece came after recalling to my counselor about many issues that I was facing. The main one was dealing with the loss of a friendship in which I had invested a great portion of me. The friendship developed by way of ministry and at the initial contact we both clicked. We did ministry together, prayed together, laughed together, and supported each other. For the first time in my adult hood, I felt like I was going to be alright and survive the scars of past failed friendships. My friend made the choice to get married and that choice produced an ill feeling within me. Partly because I knew the timing was bad and mostly because I did not like the way the fiancée treated my friend. It was not right. I talked with my friend about it, but the decision to get married was already made. I was hurt because I knew that I was losing my friend, who not only had we shared much together, but I also loved. The marriage caused my friend to leave our friendship, but I never left the friendship.

While talking about this, I realized that I was still suffering behind this loss. I was waiting for the return on my investment in the friendship. The love for my friend never ceased and I kept the door open waiting for the return of my friend. My counselor spoke and at the same time the LORD revealed to me that what I was feeling, He was feeling. God the Father has invested so much of Himself and His love into the salvation of man, by giving His only begotten Son, with the hopes that man will return to Him and the fellowship that He desires. It is sad to say, that many have not returned to Him, but He still has the door open and waiting because of the love He has for you.

This revelation changed my life forever. I have a greater love and passion for God and I made the decision to stay in fellowship with Him. I am happy to admit, that to this day, I am still waiting on the return of my friend. However, today I am not suffering from the lack that the friendship produced! The LORD has filled the void with Himself, by His Spirit and His Word. As well, He has allowed me to make many new and wonderful friends with whom I share all of that which I shared with my friend on whom I am still waiting. I am happy!

This Christmas
By: LaMont Walker

Hmmm…Christmas was different this year
It was a lot more enjoyable and filled with cheer.
I arose and slowly began the day
But I forgot to mention the toast
That my mom, sister, step-dad and I made.
We celebrated new life and family
And we expressed our joy at the Christening service for Harmony.

Mom and I danced after the sermon
Because I felt a tugging and a yearning.
Dinner was shared by all who had to offer,
Themselves and smiles was all that was needed.
I visited my cousins as family left,
I'm always to the last to come and last to leave;
But the first shall be last and the last shall be first.

I went to the movies with my sister and friends
And my puppy lover begged me to no end.
So many boys in the theater presented themselves as machos,
But my little puppy love wanted some nachos.
The love was flattering and almost scary
Because another found interest in me and her name wasn't Mary.

Yeah, this Christmas was definitely unusual.
No snow, sadness or frowns, everything was casual.
This Christmas was certainly pleasurable
And next year's won't even be measurable
I love my life and I love my savior,
I'll make it into heaven because the blood became my waiver.

This Smile

By: Lyrikal Virtuoso

Behind this smile resides tears never fallen/A heart calling to be lifted from the depths in which its crawlin/A being afraid of being because I am what I'm not supposed to be /Or so they tell me/A leader, a follower, an author of dreams/A believer in doubt, a survivor by any means/Full of rage at this world for not knowing me/Yet judging me by the external appearance you primarily see/But beyond the surface is me/Who loves being in love with the thought of one day being in love instead of being trapped in this illusion/Living in confusion/Believing in delusions that you created in my mind/While using love to blind/I now recognize your games, your tricks, your schemes (Played ever so well)/Taking over my dreams and poisoning my non-existent reality/Reducing my pride to bestiality/Now here I remain/Still the same/Unable to change/With a mind deranged and a bleeding heart from your hands/Getting over you and over us...I can/But behind.

Internal Pieces

By: LaMont Walker

Deep within the dust & clay
Are found small particles that lay.
That lay in the unseen hands of the One Creator
Who said, "I'll be back," like the terminator.
These pieces were from a heart that had already been cracked,
And shattered from life's train wreck when the car jump the track.
Internally the pieces were falling fast
While externally I was wearing my mask.

Let people see the real me and the real hurt,
Was too much risk, especially since several wanted to flirt.
That would be all that they would need
Is to see that internally I was about to bleed.
The suffering, the pain, loss of blood
Seemed to all come at me like a rushing flood.
The winds were strong, the tides were high,
And I couldn't feel a life line near by.

I could still feel these unseen hands deep within
And piece by piece I felt love being put back in.
I don't want to love because it can be so devastating,
"But you must love because you have a wife, a family, & a people waiting."
That was a sound that came from another realm, another place
Somewhere in people's mind is outer space.
I know Who said it.
I know why it was said,
But the fact of the matter was that I wanted to be dead.

"You shall live & not die!"

And again I felt this love, but this time it made me cry.

I cried because I could feel new life being created,

And from all of the previous relational hurricanes I had been emancipated.

At the moment I realized it my heart began to pump new blood.

I knew like a heart transfusion there had to be a price,

But it had already been paid by Christ when He made the ultimate sacrifice.

Internal pieces.

One More Day Before the New Year

By: LaMont Walker

One more day before the New Year
And after all that's been done,
I haven't consumed any beer.
Trust me; I've had more than a fare share,
But just what does that mean?
What is fair when you're suffering?
How do you ration out pain?
Is it possible to determine the number of tears one must shed?
And again, it's one more day before the New Year
And I find myself searching the land for cheer.

Little brother graduating high school,
Me being ordained enlarged the fire like fuel.
A niece by the name of Harmony
Brought much joy to the Walker family.
Graduation no.2,
Only this time it's big brother and the University of Missouri.
Next is Rookie to walk out free
And Tish will walk out too from high school and into liberty.

There is much to be grateful for
And much more to be completed;
Nothing can stop you when you know your enemy is defeated.
Finally, one more day before the New Year
And I have no regrets about all of the good things accomplished this year!
May your new and upcoming days be bright,
Let them bring you satisfaction and much delight!
Smile every time you open your eyes
And thank God that you're still alive.
Remember as each day passes

That it's one more day down before the New Year.

Again

By: Lamont Walker

Again, here in this place wishing I could see my face
Wandering, really wanting others to understand my base.
Base is home plate and home is where the heart is
But this heart has found itself in a position,
Position of transition here in this place again.

Again, this all seems too familiar.
I do know this one and I forgot about that one,
While the others vaguely plague my recollections.
"Hi! My name is Mr. Inspection and I have no tricks, gadgets, or magic,
Just the training and experience of life hoping that the ending isn't tragic."

Again, wanting to love and be loved for me and not for what you can see,
Tell me crystal ball…what do you see?
Truth be told, you see nothing for you have no eyes
And without sight you and others would be forced to tell lies.
Lies, deception, and defeat seem to keep surrounding me.

Again, I fight, I push, and pray with all my might
To keep fuel in the fighter plane so it will stay a flight
But the emotion and the power of love seems
To be so much more stronger and again I say,
The plight continues as I go quietly into the night.

Moving Forward

By: Alyse Fitzpatrick

Looking at myself, I'm surprised at what I see

This life I used to lead now is leading me

Seeing now why God said I need to watch and pray

Threw that sin out last week only to pick it back up today

Like trying to wear some clothes that I've already outgrown

It just doesn't fit, need to leave that old life alone

Wanting to move on, but it seems I'm being held back

Wanting to give it all to God, but feels like there's something I lack

I keep doing the things I don't want to do

My soul is screaming, it wants to honor You

It's a constant battle I that I fight

But I won't grow weary, knowing the end is almost in sight

Never knew my mind and spirit could be so conflicting

Didn't realize sin could be so addicting

There is one thing I do know, even when I don't feel it

That the Lord is sovereign and on his throne is where he sits

He rules and reigns and sees everything that's going on

He is always right here with me, even when it appears that He is gone

I know that I can stand on his promises like a bridge over the water

And let God mold me because he's the potter

So right now I guess I'll just wait, see where we go from here

Because I don't know what to do, my future is unclear

For the time being I'm leaning on the Lord, I have no fear

Because when I cry out to Him, he holds every single tear

I'm feeling Him gently guiding me back on straight and narrow

How could He not care about me when his eye is even on the sparrow

It's great to know into Gods arms I can run

Even after I acted like the prodigals son

All this time, I had been blind to all the holy spirit's hints

Now I see that God was carrying me, there's only one set of footprints

So I rebuke the devil, leaving all that sin behind
And I'm moving forward in life, no more pushing rewind.

Brain Dead

By: LaMont Walker

Trying not to think

Because it makes me sink.

Deep into the recesses of my mind

Where the activity of the past makes me wish I were blind;

Not to physical visions I see before me now

But to the actions that lead to the question how?

How did I end up here again?

How could I have been so stupid?

How did I forget?

How could I ignore it?

How could I forgive?

Forgive who? You? Not you, but me.

Loneliness causes my heart to be in despair.

Not for me, but for another.

Yeah, for another whom I've grown to love

And I hope that the hook up was from above.

If I couldn't think, this silence wouldn't stink.

The quietness of my past

Doesn't seem to last;

Last any longer than a second it seems

As I'm unable to determine the meaning of these dreams.

I still feel the touch on my right thigh

Causing me to wish I were up high.

My brain won't stop because it's not design to do so.

If my brain were dead, there would be no signals;

Instructing my tear ducts to fill and overflow.

Flow to the point of no return, causing my face to burn.

The rubbing of the nose and eyes

Makes me remember not to tell lies.

To myself first and then to another.

I couldn't feel the sharp piercing as that of a pencil lead

If I couldn't think and my brain were dead.

9 What's & 3 Whys

By: LaMont Walker

What's wrong with me?

I'm attracted to what distracts me from my destiny.

What's wrong with me?

I talk and try to find comfort in this one who's not weary.

What's wrong with me?

My desire was and is to be with you until eternity?

What's wrong with me?

My eyes often catch the images of those thrown from the wavy sea.

What's wrong with me?

I can't seem to gain any ground with the one who wants me.

What's wrong with me?

To me what's right is hard and what's wrong is easy.

What's wrong with me?

It seems that the one who doesn't deserve it, always gets it.

What's wrong with me?

I try to give away only what I should give to You.

What's wrong with me?

With the way the people around me respond,

This is the only question floating in the pond.

Being pulled from several angles,

Makes me want to strangle;

Strangle that which is precious to me.

Why do you keep pulling at me?
I can't be with you.

Why do you insist on smiling at me?
I cannot go home with you.

Why did you agree to be with me?
That experience has forever changed my necessity.
My need is for The One and only Antidote;
Please come and rescue me from this terrible mote.

One Week

By: Lamont Walker

How could this be?

Oh no…not again.

Just six days ago I was sitting on cloud nine

But was I actually there or pretending to be fine?

Spending over six rides having a conversation

With an invisible person only to end up with frustration.

That day passed and I woke up the next and put on my mask

Going undetected all the time wishing that I had a flask.

So lunedi came only to find out from a sweet voice

That whether or not of coming to a familiar place was a choice.

The following day, two's was the number I could have denied twice

But my body was not up for the fight of denying what would have been nice.

Sitting on the hump seemed to have brought some sense of happiness

Spending time with those whose time is spent in class relentlessness

Finally allowing the dog to catch up with the car that's wet

And like a school of fish being caught up in the net, I spoke.

The words were very familiar because I had spoken them before;

They bounced around from wall to wall each time begging for more;

More space to fill that hollow place so that they would mean nothing each time spoken.

Just like yesterday…she spoke words that served no purpose to another

Who I'm sure sensed the indefinite definition of the words like that of a mother.

So, they're not like you and they're not like me,

But that's no reason to treat them without respect & disregard their humanity.

Certain people are the funniest, but yet the meanest at the same time.

I said goodbye to one and hi to an ex like the next and my heart was sad

Being awakened at 1:45 in the morning of long distance by one who was mad.

Drama baby, drama, some people don't know how to live with it

And some don't know how to live.

Caught in the center of the triangle…Goodbye, hi, and why. YES BABY!

I know you've been there before….

When you've had to make all three statements at the same time;

Spending all that you have only to end up down to your last dime.

Hmmm….I keeps this piece close to me like that of my niece

As I attempt to endure this day hoping that all the pain would cease.

This is Why

By: LaMont Walker

This is why I stopped
Just like a stomach to a rollercoaster
Instantly my heart was dropped.

This is why I stopped
Like too much helium in a balloon
The emotion of anger had popped.

This is why I quit
So that I wouldn't be sad
And have to buy clothes I couldn't fit.

This is why I quit
So that I wouldn't be like an item in antique store
Not knowing my value and having to sit.

This is why I cried
Because like water to a sponge
The love in my heart had all dried.

This is why I cried
Because like paint to parchment
The life was dull and confused on the inside.

This is why I choose to say Goodbye,
So that my heart can beat again
And my emotional man be released to sigh.

This is why I choose to say Goodbye,
So that you might save your sorry goodbye's

And never be forced again to create a lie!

MUTE CONFESSIONS

By: Lyrikal Virtuoso

My eyes tell a story unseen/ blind to the world/ yet so visible to me/ saddened by what I see/ viewing my life repeatedly/ while my ears hear the cries of the innocent child I used to be/ deaf to the world/ but loud and clear to me/ tears heavy with pain and grief/ while my lips remain sealed because of fear and disbelief/ mute to the world/ but outspoken to me/ holding on to those words, that at that time, I couldn't speak/ my body's weak/ from losing blood that my heart began to leak/ every minute, day, and week/ my mind continued to seek/ for an outlet or release/ that would reveal the unique side of me/ these thoughts/ dumb to the world/ but so intelligent to me/ then my hands revealed this technique/ that no one could critique/ paralyzed to the world/ but so active to me/ so now I write all those things that I hear, think and see...

From the Shadows of Darkness

By: Lamont Walker

Passing through the valley of shadows
Where there seems to be no grass or green meadows
The sounds coming from this dark place without light
Seem to be created from beings who struggle with right.
Without any light wrong continues to remain in the night
In the light of this night are the fears of these creations
Hurting from the past mistakes and present ill conditions.
As I continue walking through this dimly lit atmosphere
I wonder what in the world am I doing here.
Ashamed, afraid, feeling like a failure and a let down
Having to wear a mask & white foundation like that of a clown
So that no one can see the imprints left on me
By those who dwell in the shadows of darkness
All the while hoping that no one discovers this is my home too.

Random Questions

By: LaMont Walker

Why did I open my mouth?

Why did I fall for my friend?

Why did I even have to say anything?

Who passed on this painful torch?

When will I sincerely be filled with happiness?

What do you do when you feel betrayed by yourself?

What do you do when you've hurt you?

How do you forgive yourself for being so stupid?

Why did I break the rules? You know the rules....

Who always ends up broken hearted with the short end of the stick?

How do I keep control over my emotions when it seems that they're spread as far
as the east is from the west?

What do you do when you've done all you can?

What do you give when you've given your all?

Most importantly right now, how do you handle the guilt of today?

Why should I luvv?

Where is my heart? I only hold fragments of it...

How could I have been so stupid?

Why does this keep happening to me in this season?

Why does depression seem to hover above me like a dark rain cloud that never
passes?

Where are my feelings? I feel nothing...numb...

Why did you find me?

How did you get inside of my mind?

Why are my thoughts filled with you?

Why am I so screwed up?

Can I trust you?

Can I just....sleep?

There is only but one answer to all of these questions;

I am an oxymoron.

I am, but I'm not.

I do, but I don't.

I will, but I won't.

I can, but I can't.

Will I do this again? The answer to that…at this point is probably yes…

Will you forgive me?

Can you walk with me?

Will you hold me?

Can you help me?

Will you judge me?

Can you cover me?

When the day is over, the question you must answer, is will you luvv me for me?

This Season

By: LaMont Walker

This season never seems to change
The same old memories with new experiences got me acting strange;
I'm up one day and down the next feeling deranged,
Wondering as the hours pass, when will this season change?

This season is a never ending repetition
Bringing all of the produce of this season to fruition.
Yes all around me is nothing but fields of rejection
Got me pretending to be a VCR with a bad tape and performing ejection.

This season causes me to sense that I'm trapped
No route, no sign, no way of escape has been mapped;
Seeming as if this can't be shook so I napped.
Around this notion I can't get my mind to be wrapped.

This season I'm in I'm trying to shape
Can't get it to flow evenly like my window's drape.
So I go to work and eat and drink my Welch's grape
Hoping everyday that I never again have to experience rape.

This never ending season has caused me to cry
Not outwardly, but inwardly wanting to die
So I'm choosing to commit suicide as I lie
Upon the altar of sacrifice He'll cause me to live high.

This season will change.
This season will end.
This season will bend and liberated me.
This season will be as gold as it, I mold.
This season will be no more tears as I progress for the rest of my years.

Identity Fraud

By: LaMont Walker

As I was sitting on the side feeling captured,
You looked into my eyes making me wish I was raptured.
Yes, caught up because I had been caught up
Moving about like a horse that would gallop.
Unbeknownst to me, I had no longer been me,
But I had become one who was not living in fantasy.
For the soothing touch I felt was real
And not knowing because of that, later my mind would need to heal.

Days, months, and years down the line
Here I am living and thinking that I'm fine;
Til you saw that I had expired in 07'
Again making me wish I was in heaven!
Feeling congested, remembering when I was arrested,
And hoping to never ever be molested.
Looking down into my existence you said I was suspended
And I had no recollection of the wrong I supposedly bended.
Calling from here and searching there
Only to conclude that I had been duplicated everywhere!
One time in Kansas and in Missouri three,
Unfortunately it wasn't for that Holy Trinity.
I got to be original for there is only one me
But because of this present condition I'm still fighting for my liberty.
Thus far I've been able to pull off layers of the plague,
Hopefully to the condition becoming more and more vague.

Now having a greater understanding that's no longer broad,
I stood before the judge to communicate identity fraud;
All the while wanting to holler drop kick em' like Jean Claude!
Ya'll one so close who lied and said it was me,

While the real me was hundreds of miles away on bended knee.

To further complicate the situation,

There were too many people I had been with in that equation.

I ended up having to do the addition and subtraction of math,

WHEW! Once I finished I felt like I needed a bath!

I needed to be cleansed, which was hard, but I admitted;

And it was all because of the identity fraud that had been committed!

Evolution

By: LaMont Walker

The process of change in a particular direction

Moving from place to place always securing my protection.

For on this path of life I've made the selection

To always heal and forgive whenever there is rejection.

Rejection was apart of the direction when suicide was an election

But because of the distance traveled the thoughts were soon followed by ejection.

There I found myself in the middle of my evolution

Not fully understanding how to come to a resolution.

In my own mind the process had begun that I like to call revolution

Yes, my thoughts began to rotate around the theory of exclusion

I had put away the truth,

Ignored my heart and followed my mind

Right down the path where the blind lead the blind…destruction.

Desperate, cold, lonely, and shattered

And often times feeling as if I had been shattered.

The need for change wasn't only immediate and expedient

I needed my sight back and the missing ingredient.

What was lacking had been found in The Three in One

Yes, some know it as The Father, Spirit, and Son.

The Father opened my eyes to see

Just how much The Son really loves me.

The rest was left to The Spirit who is the best

At leading all in the path of righteousness with zest!

The winds of change had blown my way

Causing me to evolve into the man that you love today.

Relationship Pieces

I luvv to hear my pastor preach about relationships because I believe that is his prophetic message to the body of Christ. Stop and think about it; the biggest headache we all have had to face is, my pastor will raise his arms, and the congregation will respond, relationships! Within the next few pieces, you will see the headache, joy, and frustration of relationships.

The Secret Unfolds

By: LaMont Walker

Hmmm….I have a secret to tell,
But it's only for those whose hearts listen well.
This secret I've suppressed for so long,
If I told it people would call me wrong.
Why should I tell you when you won't believe me?
When deep inside you really want to be me.

It goes a little something like this,
My heart fainted because of a passionate kiss.
For the first time in my life, I thought I knew love.
I felt accepted for me and not for some fake wanna be.
I could relax and be the real me.
The real me, the real me.

No haters, perpetrators, impersonators of any sort,
Just me is all I wanted to be.
So I took the chance to be free,
But I never ever knew true liberty.
The secret is this and I'll let you go,
He loved me 1st and I'll never say no.

You Loved Me

By: LaMont Walker

When I first met you, you told me you loved me.

I had just met you, so how could you love me?

I was stupid in my head

And all you wanted was me in your bed.

"No it's not that way, I really love you!"

You didn't even know my middle name, favorite color, or even that my
eyes were brown,

But you love me?

So a few days later, I risk loving you back

Because I thought you were real.

Oh how that backfired in my face

As you told me how you feel.

I cried, I died, I committed suicide

And it still hadn't ended

Because my heart you never mended.

As I packed my bags,

The tears strolled down my face

And then I heard a voice that said,

"I AM in this place."

I turned and I looked and there was nobody but me

And then I felt a fresh wind all over my body.

I felt comfort, I felt peace.

My troubled mind was put at ease, at ease, at ease.

I realized Who it was that was speaking to me.

It was the One who died on that old rugged tree.

And I asked how could this be?

And You said You did it

All because You loved me, You loved, You loved me.

Internal pieces of 'You Loved Me':

The story behind this piece is clearly one of hurt and reassurance. Often times the desire of a relationship causes one to be blind to the obvious signs of destruction that await a relationship born out of lust. I lusted for a relationship and I got one...with the wrong person and at the wrong time! I had opened myself to this individual who was working to fulfill their own selfish desires. It was some years before I found that out and it came to me because I met another victim of that predator. I opened my heart and in I allowed this person. No sooner than I had done that, they were standing in front of me saying they did not want me or the relationship.

I became sick. I was physically sick and homesick because I was in college at the time. While in my dorm, I looked out the window and the sun was shining so bright, the sky was a beautiful blue and the weather was good for summer time fun. None of that was able to change the way I felt inside. Tears were coming down my face due to the pain and my only thought was to end it all. Yes, thoughts of suicide were forming in my mind and I started the plans for execution. While I was packing my bags and tears still streaming down, I heard the soft voice of the LORD speak and remind me of His promise that He will never leave me or forsake me. Immediately afterwards there was a wind that came over my body and the only thing I could do was lie down in the peace and comfort that it brought. God the Father reminded me that He loves me more than anyone! After repenting for my lust, I have been blessed to never return to that dark place mentally or emotionally. Now, I run out when the sky is blue and have fun in the sun because God loves me and I love Him!

I Left You

By: LaMont Walker

Today I love you.
Tomorrow, I liked you.
The day after, well you didn't exist.
You see, as the future came closer,
Our happily ever after began to fade.
What a relief in my mind
Because you really had me in a bind.
I couldn't love, eat, think or drive
Until in me you came all the way live.

Today is gone and tomorrow never came.
The day after, everything stayed the same.
You still called, I smelled your scent and my heart was rent.
After long conversations, you never even knew what I meant.
To bypass the ignorance, misunderstandings and confusion,
I transcended to a place far beyond any illusion.
I went to a place that you'll never visit soon.
It's a dark place where the sun shines and it's called the moon.

I went there because I could relate.
It's always hanging around in the sky,
But it's never seen until the sun is nigh.
I'm always hanging around other people,
But I'm not noticed until you're there.
Some times the moon is full and some times it's not.
I'm full when you're there, but empty quite a lot.

So I gave up on time and went to that place,
To a place without time and nothing but just space.

You may think nothing of this

And that is fine.

It just proves that you still drink from ignorance's glass of wine.

The You in Me

By: LaMont Walker

I met you today
Though I saw you last week
And every since then,
It was you my heart set out to seek.
As you walked by
My pupils caught your eyes
And I saw deep into your soul
As we exchanged our hi's.

The passion in your voice quickly connected to me fine
And I felt the hands of your emotions caressing mine.
If I could turn back time
I would have you do it again,
But I didn't have to because you did.
This time it was deeper.

I saw you from a distance walking slowly
And I followed every footstep lowly.
I stepped where you had marked with your footprints
Until at last again the windows of your soul sensed,
Sensed me that is.
I walked by you
Again, and again, and again
Each time hoping that you would touch me without your hands.
YES! I was successful because I found out your homelands.

As I left you, I hoped our paths were a figure 8
So as I skate and jump you'll never be late!
You will walk around, lie around, and talk all night
And you'll do it all without your legs, a bed, and phone in sight!

Let Me In

By: LaMont Walker

Open up and please let me in
Your heart's desire I want to win.
I look at you and hope for a smile
You challenge me to go an extra mile.
Why are you so solid like a brick?
Do you think on you I'll play a trick?
I try over and over again to get in,
But I'm like a baby seeing all the rooms in a house,
And realizing that I'm trapped by a play-pin.
Let me in the room where you live
And all that I have, I'll give.
Let me in the room where you dine,
And I'll let you drink of joy's bottomless glass of wine.
Let me in the room where you rest your head
And I'll cover you like the sky covers the sea that's red.

I am filled with excitement while in your presence.
I try to keep from smiling on the outside,
When on the inside I WANT YOU I cried.
Oh if only you could understand my feelings!
If you knew my insides were exploding for you,
How would you respond?
Even now I wish you were here.
In my mind you're always near.

So I'm standing and waiting at the door of your heart
Wondering will you let me in?

FREE of You

By: LaMont Walker

Boy, am I free of you!

Humph…and to think, you, I was trying to woo!

I would call and inquire about your day,

Your feelings, mental state and try to speak your troubles away.

I visited you and kept you company.

How stupid was I to desire your companionship.

I sincerely sought you out and was willing to give you whatever,

But you were too blind by your own fatal attraction to self.

You never really listened to me.

How I do know? Your own lips secretly told me so.

Argh! Why did I waste my time with you?

Tell me that! Let's talk about reality!

Now that I'm free of you, I see your life in a new light.

Boo, you're living a boring life.

You're searching for reality in fantasy.

Snap out of the trance of lies!

Eww…you almost had me caught up in soul-ties!

But baby, I'm free of you! Hear me roar!

Hercules, I'm free of you!

Ashteroth, I'm definitely free of you!

Blue, I'm free of you!

WWF, I'm certainly free of you!

Ford Mustang, I'm totally free of you!

Anger, hallelujah I'm free of you!

Deathly Pleasurable
By: LaMont Walker

I've been wanting to cry every since
A few days ago the increase in my sense
Brought to my understanding these thoughts.
These thoughts I'd quickly comprehend
Was a reality that I had been living in.
The chambers where love flows are dark.
Deep reds and burgundies fill the walls
A mixture of love and hate I see as I walk the halls.
A strong desire just to be with who
And the possibility increases each time I think of you.

You come with grace notes and the exoticism of the French
And you come with the trills and excitement of the Italians.
Then I think to myself…
Imperfect in all of my humanity
Yet striving to keep my dignity.
Even while the many others disgrace my discipline
I try to walk the line between satisfaction and sin.
Sin is ever present and I wish I weren't
Because everywhere I am, it shows up.
Good morning!
Let's have lunch!
Call me tonight!
Punch it 90 mph!
Let's sleep!
Why can't I seem to escape you?
My flesh craves what brings it death
And the pleasure it produces takes my very breath.
Tell the undertaker to prepare for my arrival

For I have tasted that which is deathly pleasurable.

Caught Up

By: Lamont Walker

Caught up in between the me and the who

Seeking, desiring, and longing for a touch, just something from who.

It seems as if at any time anybody will suffice

But because of my dignity and wisdom I'm only willing to sacrifice;

Sacrifice little because of the popularity

And at any given moment the truth will pop open reality.

The reality of this fantasy includes too many of you;

Like in a sea with many schools of fish

I sit, I look, I wait and I ponder, while at the same making my wish.

I wish I could fish for the one who would dish what I would wish;

But even with the dish there are still too many schools of fish.

Cat, perch, trout, and salmon

And not enough worms or lines to draw them into the in between.

The sight of the tails of the waving in the crystal blue waters

Causes me to stray away from the desire of two daughters.

You splish and I splash and when nets are dropped we both make a dash.

I laugh out loud and act as to make you tickle

But if the hook ever sank in we would be in a pickle.

Now being and existing in this time of in between,

Causes me to crave and ache for even some times dream.

I could sit with you and be with you every day of the week

And time after time again regaining strength to have because I'm weak.

I can't stay here with you because you have made your pledge;

So in my disposition I'll remain stuck here between this wedge.

The Unspoken Request

By: LaMont Walker

Speaking but no sound comes out
And the message is heard by those whose hearts are turned about
The combinations of adjectives and verbs
Are hoped to be preserved like that of herbs.
Line by line, and word by word
The meaning became quite clear by the more that was heard
It asked of one simple request
And that was not to be hurt by the one who is the best
Thirty-one is unbelievable
And two elevens are inconceivable
But only one is uncontrollable…Love
Can't control the love I have for you
While at the same time trying to keep you in view
The heart is heavy with thought of psyche
But hoping to give them away to Mikey
They say he'll eat anything
But his system can't digest this wing
On the wings of love I want to fly
For there no hurt is near by
No hurt, no pain, no agony
Is the song of this tall canapé
The pieces of this heart has just been sorted
Please lose your flexibility so they're not contorted
No walls built and no high vaults
All blame falls on one and that's whose fault,
Please stop poking my eyes because you see the tears
It took some time to dry them up and let it be for years
This is the unspoken request.

The Unexpected

By: LaMont Walker

How could this be?
Living in a new realm of reality,
I never knew this life existed
And I'm glad my heart didn't resist it.
Here I experience so many pleasurable emotions
And I hope to never endure any demotions.
Just how did I arrive to this place undetected?
It was by one that I've come to know as the Unexpected.

You came into my life and I didn't know it
Until you called my name and I couldn't hold it
I couldn't hold the proper response for one such as you
For when I realized it, my tenebrous skies turned blue
The light in your eyes showed me I was not at my demise
As a new journey of life I should not despise.

It seems as if out of nowhere you came along
And snatched me up in your arms where there's no wrong.
Trying to pinpoint the exact meeting joint,
So that an anniversary of newness might be celebrated.
Unable to determine when, and to date still no sin
Both of us remembering a piece here and a piece there
While we remain caught up in this place with luvv everywhere.

I had no idea that luvv'n like this would be
And even better, your luvv has surrounded and engulfed me.
Feeling like the warm sand in between toes on a beach
Soothing to the sense of touch and eager for you to reach;
Reach out and hold me and never let me go
Because deep inside of me is a never ending flow.

I let the flow go because you know how to row.

Row, row, row ya boat gently down the stream

Merrily, merrily, merrily, merrily, I'm glad this ship's not a dream.

Oh no! For the captain and his sailor are alive and well

Exchanging in conversation, each hoping the other will tell;

Tell of the secret treasures that you've hidden

Let me explore every inch and leave nothing forbidden.

Before, I was just the captain, but now I've become a sailor

And I'm luvv'n the ride and praying that I never become a jailor.

Please don't lock me up, unless it's in your arms.

Please don't lock me up, unless it's in your love.

Please don't lock me up, unless it's in your mind.

I hadn't expected for you to be with me

But oh the glory since you've come!

Please say that you'll stay until eternity!

The Unexpected arrival has caused me to cry

Because I feel like I can breathe again and release a sigh.

For I had held my breath and I was dying and didn't know it

Suffocating from a lack of oxygen trying not to blow it.

1,2,3,4, you knew how to breathe into me making me want more

Please give me more of your time

Please give me more of your mind

Please give me more of your...rhyme.

The Unexpected has opened my eyes, now I can see

The level of real luvv waiting inside of me.

A new David & Jonathan have been released!

I luvv the Unexpected more than you'll ever know!

For those that want to sit, the Unexpected will answer you NO!

Here's to the Unexpected!

I luvv you forever...

You Got Me

By: Lyrikal Virtuoso

...wonderin how I can get to that state of BE...where we can BE...in that place of fantasy...trying to figure out how to make this dream survive the death of me awaking...searching for words to mold the sense that I'm making...faking happiness with them when it's YOU...that got me...

Tangled up in non-existent words...letters...phrases yet to be put together...focusing on that invisible focus some type of hocus pocus that got me jinxed...seeing only you in a world of billions but like a chameleon I hide...from YOU...who got me...feelin...a thousand feelings and still trying to figure how all my emotions just survived this head on collision...no scratches...no bruises...no pains or contusions cause you...who got me

Seeing illusions as real, amazing me with ur ability to heal a heart like mine wounded over the years...you're like my "white-lighter" healing the "charmed one" from the demon's slay...taking away the power of 3 and replacing the power of me with the power of you...who...GOT me...

Chasing your image in a world of white...hoping we clash to bring forth the colors of earth on this canvas of life...on one knee hoping to one day ask u to be my...

...it's me you got...all of me that I know...and all of me that I discover in daily sorrows, but yours to have, and mine to borrow...faint memories of you clearly existing in the air's fog that follows...life's rains from the sky's pains, falling like an ocean that's all too much to contain in the space of a sea...finding comfort in the "uneasy" cause I know...that YOU...got me...

Consumption

By: LaMont Walker

This is more than a crush…

It's a fantasy, a reality, leading up to eternity

An eternal place of bliss and passion

Enjoying the sounds of the waves crashing

Such a place never found a lashing,

And the thoughts of you, I'm never bashing.

I'm insane in my mem brain when I call yo' name

And I can't fake it, can't shake it,

I'm a have to have you so I can make it!

This tension keeps causing an extension

And your touch and I can't even mention!

Sitting here hoping and praying that you would dish,

What I would wish without the school of fish!

When I stop to look up and I see the expression on your face,

Your words, your movements, and your looks shatter this place!

Yes, this place on the inside and in the present tense,

Where the feelings of mutual that you now currently sense!

You sensed passion, desire, appeal and attraction

Each hoping that you would stop and give a reaction!

Extend the invitation to each and let's stop hiding in the clear,

Because the pink note, pink slip indicated how I wanted you near!

Your eyes have captured me by fashion;

Your arms so strong pull me in by dashing;

I'm hooked…….

Like a fish I've yanked, I've squirmed, and tried to get free

But your entire existence keeps squeezing me!

It's no fair being in a place with much space and no race,

So set the pace and I'll seek ya face

And around you with my arms I'll lace.

I'm trapped in a room with no gloom and only hope!

Come be my knight in shining armor and help me to cope!

I've got the lock and you've got the key,

Won't you please come and rescue me!?!?

If I'm correct, I end with this assumption,

Soon, with thoughts, words, and touches of me will be your consumption!

Be, I'm consumed!

You, Me, We, & All

By: Lyrikal Virtuoso

My self-mutilation is a result of my irritation from your daily self-presentations/Imitating what I thought was right /until my eye took sight of that darker bright/ side of you/You...the one that my "all" was wrapped around/not realizing till now/that you kept my "all" bound/clearly now/I can see/that my "all" shoulda been wrapped around Me/But "we" was all I thought there could be/Until finally/"Me" deceased/Leaving "we" to be You/and "all" became nothing

Conversations

By: LaMont Walker

I opened my ear and I heard many conversations
Ranging from topics of love, hate, bitterness, and freedom.

Hey boo! How was your day?
It really doesn't matter because I'm going to romance you anyway.
Baby my day was long and stressful
But I didn't want to fill your cup with all of that,
So I gave it a letter of dismissal.
Honey I'm glad you did because I plan to guide you to where love is overflowing,
This atmosphere is only reached by those who remain in the knowing.
Knowing what you want and persevering until you obtain it
Even if that means searching the entire planet.

Ew I really hate her! She did me wrong and she knew it!
What happened?
As I tried to the strongest of my ability
She said that I was full of futility.
After she said that, what happened?
Anger rose from deep within me
And I told her everything that I would endeavor to be.
I told her I would be successful at everything I attempt,
Because in Him there is no failure and He's made me stronger than any wimp!
Not that I would pimp, walk with a limp
But that my fame and fortune would be known and visible like the Goodyear blimp!

I'm not mad as hell! I'm full of bitterness!
He lied to me from the very beginning like a backstabbing friend,
He talked with a smooth voice just long enough to woo me in.
I walked through the door and I couldn't resist those thick juicy lips,

Before I could even speak they had already moved to my hips.

The night was unforgettable and the morning after made it worse.

I found out that after I had left his house he had worked a curse.

A curse to keep me from the knowing the truth

That I was only one of the many peanuts in that Babyruth.

Once I found that out, I never forgave him and I started to clog on the inside,

But I was determined to remain dignified and not lose my sense of pride.

I'll call you again very soon.

The guard is telling me that it's time to sing another tune.

I got out today! I'm FREE!

All because I went to a church where the Spirit of God touched me.

It felt so familiar but I didn't know it.

Strange huh? But I didn't care!

I just knew that I was glad to be there!

I was released into a place that I had never experienced.

My eyes were wide opened and to my recollection,

I never left the room of the congregation.

The preacher said your hungry soul He'll feed

And whom the Son has set free is free indeed!

I didn't know what any of that meant at the time,

But for what it was worth, I was a candidate known as prime.

Yes the right target for the Word to hit

Because all of the chains had become so perfectly knit.

I couldn't move as fast as I wanted to, but I made it to the altar.

I asked God for forgiveness of my sins

And the pastor told me that God had already cleansed!

I was free from the taint and all of the filth that I ate,

I instantly started losing all of the unnecessary weight!

Dear diary, I got free!

I am free!

And I will forever be FREE!

Pieces of Luvv

Luvv is not easy to define and luvv certainly is not an easy thing to do. However, we all need it and want it and no one can resist real luvv. It is time for a little romanticism.

Love Speaks

By: LaMont Walker

1st

A thought in my mind came through
Reminisced when I first met you
Tenebrous skies turned blue
Felt too good to be true
Someone whose love is real
Though intangible I can feel
Strong as silk from the land
Imprints my heart like sand

2nd

Eyes open now I can see
I was lost in reality
Living in fantasy
Pleasing all but who cares for me
Deep was the pain you felt
Causing your heart to melt
Quickly to the rescue
Passion was soon renewed

Speak, love speak
You've waited so long
To express these words
Opportunity's here
Speak loud and clear

I'm here before you
With an open heart
Ready to journey with a fresh start

A brand new heart and a brand new love
I offer you

I present my body as a living sacrifice
On Calvary's cross you paid the price
A brand new heart and a brand new love
I offer you

Love Lifted Me

By: LaMont Walker

I was wrapped up, tied up tangled up
In a world of sin, I had no peace within
I was looking, for love in the wrong place
When true love, was staring me in the face

I found Him in time
He delivered my mind
Soul has been refined
Just in time

The true love, that my heart has finally found
Set my, spirit free when I was bound
Now He fills me up, till the brim of my cup
Begins to overflow, with His everlasting love

I found Him in time
He delivered my mind
Soul has been refined
Just in time

Love lifted me
Love lifted me
When nothing else could help
Love lifted me

Love lifted me
So glad that love lifted me
When nothing else could help
Love lifted

Love lifted me

God's love lifted me

Internal Pieces of 'Love Lifted Me":

I decided to turn this piece into a song that I have loved since I have written it! I was at a point trying to find satisfaction of myself and life. I did this through sexual immorality, alcohol, partying with friends, do what others wanted me to do in hopes that it would please them, still thinking that I would be satisfied. There was one thing that remained constant, and that was at the end of each act, I was still at the bottom in my emotions and self-esteem.

Taking a moment to observe why I found myself constantly at the bottom of life, I discovered the reason. I was ignoring my relationship with God. I was not totally ignoring Him, just not giving Him 100% attention and time. I would go to church and sing, dance, pray, and play and immediately afterwards return to my quest of finding satisfaction. I understood that I invested more in these temporary things and not enough in the things that are eternal, like my soul and spirit. I picked up my Bible and read something in Jeremiah 31 that said, "I have loved thee with an everlasting love" and in Matthew 28 it said "I am with you always even until the end." It was then that it came to me that the Father's love is everlasting and always present. How exciting that was to me! His love was what I had not pursued. Once I did, the satisfaction that is now within me, is indescribable! The only thing I can encourage you to do is Psalm 34:8 "O taste and see that the Lord is good!" (KJV)

Loved to Death

By: LaMont Walker

Here we are together again.

You've grown to be quite a tasteful asset.

Every time we're together,

I'm forced to love you to death.

I love you so much

That I would reverse the world for you.

Every time I look into the windows of your soul,

I always find a new piece of coal.

And I die again because of the love I have for you.

I want to be with you, but it's impossible.

To you, I'm just another thing to do.

You didn't even know that I died

Because my love for you I denied.

I denied it so much until it became null,

And once that happened I had no feeling,

Which meant no heart beat.

No heart beat, heart beat, heartbeat.

Resulting in only one thing, death.

I searched and I searched for another opportunity to live,

But soon determined that I had no more to give.

All of the love that I had, I gave to you.

Hoping for reciprocation, you never came through.

So there I sat in death, miserable.

And listened to the stories that erected feelings I hate,

By all of the others who had met the same fate.

Signed,

Loved to Death

A Four Letter Desire

By: LaMont Walker

Longing to be with you
But my heart you never knew.
Having the truth of reality makes me feel blue.
This thing, feeling, action, and emotion
All wrapped up in four little letters.

I could easily pronounce it
But you wouldn't even announce it.
Who came up with it?
Who taught the first lesson on it?
How do some fakes act it out,
But the genuine always find its route?

Bass guitar will you please talk to me?
Tell me of your innermost secret
And I'll keep it safe inside of me, me, and me.
Pick a fret and play a melodious chord,
The more you share I promise to never get bored.
Oh how I long to hear your tune
Because in the middle of winter I'm reminded of June.

One more time bass guitar,
I promise to be gentle if your heart's ajar.
I hear your low strings being plucked by strong hands
And your high strings are in demand.
So play for me this four letter word.
Sing to me about this four letter word.
Finally, talk, to me about this four letter word.

Smiles

By: LaMont Walker

Smiling on the inside is my heart
And it happens every time I'm around you.
The reason it smiles
Is because your heart has made it glad.
Your thought connected to mine,
The vibe I sent you made you respond with,
I'm fine.

I'm fine because you're here
And I know you'll take me to that special place you hold dear.
Right you are, because I want you there.
When you're there, I know you're safe.
In that place you're free to express your true identity.
I know when you're here, you never fear.
Fear that if you smile it won't be returned.
Oh no, when you smile, my heart thumps twice.
Once for you and once for me.
When you smile there,
I'm giving you life in exchange for another smile.

Please keep smiling so that I won't die.
Let your heart be merry and filled with glee
So that I may smile into eternity.

Power of Touch

By: Poetry in Motion

Oh if my lips could touch your lips

How my mind would reminisce on the day when a kiss was yet so innocent

Not trying to be your man but loving you for more than just a friend

Oh if my lips could touch your lips

How the anticipated shock would flow through me

Like rain on a cold autumn's eve

Oh if my lips could touch your lips

How my heart would sound like

Wave crashing against the sore

Like a high tide from a lunar eclipse

Oh if my lips could touch your lips

I would be the instrument and you would be the soloist

Melodically exploring the octave and scales of my love and emotions

A Rose

By: Poetry in Motion

A is for the Almighty who made you in His divine image

R is for your Radiant beauty that can only be compared to watching a morning sunrise

O is for Others have tried to approach you but yet your value is set to high

S is for the Sweet aroma of your presence that fills the room when you walk by

E is for an Evening of watching your personality blossom

Like the red, the white, and yellow of peddles of

A Rose

LostInYourLove

By: LaMont Walker

Where am I?

For I have found myself looking around

Hearing no voices but a familiar sound

Searching for a way to begin on the path

Considering everybody else and their feelings in the aftermath;

I start to walk the trail that you've made

And your feelings and my feelings of emptiness starts to fade;

Fearlessly going along this way

And I pass a frame with you and I say,

Say that you'll stop by again with your smile

Because I'm always empowered and feel like the extra mile.

Moving forward and I sense a strong touch

A message from you came to my heart that said I love you much!

Still unsure of where I am and how I got here,

Not knowing if I should turn back or hold you dear.

There is one thing that I know for certain,

And that is I could perceive that love was near.

As a matter of fact, I looked towards the sky

And I saw your love on a dove flying high;

I waved my hands and felt something warm

It was the breath of your love that said I'll never harm.

So I continued on this journey not knowing where to go.

I'm lost in this place that I call your love

And I know your eyes are leading me to a place I don't know of.

Being in this place has put an everlasting smile on my face

Knowing that I'm inside of you, this love space

Causes my heart to race at a pace to your base.

My conclusion is, this is it…I'm lost and at peace.

Your love feeds me, covers me, clothes, me and holds me.

From you nor this I cannot turn away

Right here, lost in your love, is where I'll forever stay!

I'm lost…

Is This Love?

By: LaMont Walker

I wake up in the morning, and I think about you.
When I go to bed at night, I think about you.
Is this love?

While I'm driving my car you're on my mind.
As I go to class, I'm thinking about you all the time.
Is this love?

When I pray, I never forget to mention you
And I thank God that our friendship is new.
Is this love?

For you I like to cook
And when we're studying, it's you I'm thinking about and not a book.
Is this love?

I never knew that meeting someone so beautiful
would come and make my thought life so wonderful.
Is this love?

I was immature before, but now I see so much more
I love it everyday, when you come my way
Just to see you smile, helps me to go another mile.
I'm not writing this to woo you in, but I now realize in you that I have a friend.

Correction is never easy to accept, but if you hadn't given it, my heart would have
wept.
It seems like these lines and rhymes, have an endless flow but now has come time
for me to go.

I feel that if you've read up to this line,
I've made my point just fine!
I conclude that this love is as pure white as a dove
and I will pursue this love until the very end.

In The Mood

By: LaMont Walker

I'm in the mood for love, joy, and victory
No more stress and drama cause I've been liberated totally.
Hold your head up high and sigh
Always remember and never forget Christ is standing by.
Today is the best day of your life
And tomorrow, though not promised,
Will bring an abundance of joy and love always missed.
I'm at this table filled with much food,
And ready to eat your love because I'm in the mood.
I love you back

Future

By: LaMont Walker

Not even knowing where to begin
I find myself contemplating from the deep recesses within
What should I do about the way that I feel?
They tell me to rest in time because there all things heal.
My heart is for two when it only should be for one
That is me, myself, and I...
But because of my make up
I have to front and put on the fake up
When the one is brought up
So that I don't get caught up
Causing me to tell the others to shut up.
Nobody knows the trouble I see
Because I'm far ahead of their game and they can't catch me
Filling your head with false hope
Not knowing eventually they'll need to throw you a rope
Calling it a life line
Because you have flat lined.
Clear...quickly they move with frantic
Simply due to the fact that you panicked
You were oh so strong in the beginning
But being too late, you pulled ya best game in the last inning.
Do I apologize for making you realize?
Will I be ostracized for giving a criticize?
Do I chase after a love that's abased?
Is this a fabrication of my imagination?
There is but only one who is the possessor
Who moves closer to me as I move towards the dresser
Dress me, bless me, caress me, don't mess me
But ease me, release me, grease me, don't decrease me.
For I'm still in a place and trying to see you face to face

And with nothing but love I hope you're laced.

I greet you with a kiss that's full of bliss…good morning Future!

Creative Pieces

I decided to dip into my imagination and well, you will see what came out. Free your mind for a mental stretching.

Breathe

By: LaMont Walker

My heart smiled all day
With passing seconds that stood still.
Thoughts of you, euphoria filled.
As I inhaled the carbon monoxide
Produced by only two lungs,
The slower my heart pumped
Because of the elongated period of waiting to inhale.

The story of challenges rides on the breath
As the vocal cords vibrate loving me to death.
Soothing sounds rode the expensive warm air
Until they reach my heart and said I saw me in there.

With each release of old wind
I felt the bonds of a new relationship bend,
Loop after loop after loop, until they were tied in a knot,
And in an internal inferno they'll remain,
Never to get hot.

Breathe, breathe, breathe.
With every inhalation I freely fly in,
First passing the shifting clay that produces pleasure
And then greeting ten of the thirty bones that guard the key.
The key that will unlock any door you want to enter.
Enter one room and you might find winter,
But enter into another and you'll reach the center.
The center where I found you and you found me.

Flaming Desire

By: LaMont Walker

This whole note is my flaming desire.
I inhaled a low breath and sang it
And suddenly sparked a fire.
This six foot fire burns with intense flames
And you can't feel it unless you call its name.

I call you whole note after your make-up.
Combinations of two half-note windows,
Four quarter-note limbs, and eight eighth-note touches
All make you whole.

Why, I desire to sing this whole note
Because of the flaming passion within.
You lie within my range,
And you know that's not strange.
A beautiful color I produce
When this whole note I sing,
If Mr. Carelessness and Mr. Bold would speak,
I would offer you a ring.

It would symbolize that you are my flaming desire
And only a kiss will tell,
Whether or not this note that I'm singing,
Will cause my heart to fail.

The Beginning Is Near the End

By: LaMont Walker

Well, this is it.

I'm at 10 and the count down has already begun.

10 classes and 20 hours I'm taking

Hoping that I'm a singer in the making.

Oh how I love to sing and that's apart of the intro

That will lead me to the end where a new life begins.

My heart and time stood still while I talked with mother,

She said that her singleness was ending due to her new found lover.

I'm, we're starting all over again as we approach the end.

I saw the bass guitar I used to play.

Ellis was the man that had it on display.

I picked it up and touched the frets.

Once I remembered the fingering positions,

It was as if I started to play a new song.

This time there were more smiles and no butterflies.

It's not until after you take the test,

That you learn how to drive your best.

It's not until you cross the platform,

That you begin to use the degree

That you've sweated for, lost sleep for, and

Fell in and out of love for.

See, the beginning is always at the end.

When one style of perception fades,

You should set a new trend.

The Fingers, The Keys, & The Ears

By: LaMont Walker

As the fingers gently played the keys,

The song that was heard truly pierced each ear.

It seemed as though the keys silently begged,

Begged the strong fingers to play any song.

"Please play a song, your hands we want to feel."

As each finger curved into position,

The listening ears waited in anticipation.

"What will we hear today?"

The fingers began to touch and speak of the song:

> This melody for you, I compose.
>
> It came from my heart I suppose
>
> Because it's filled with love, compassion, and hope.
>
> Hoping that you will be mine,
>
> That I may love on, in, and through you.
>
> Showing you compassion your mind never knew.
>
> This melody for you is simple
>
> So that you will clearly hear the message.
>
> You are my inspiration, motivation, and activation.
>
> Let the waves of sound
>
> Swiftly carry this message to you
>
> That I may no longer cry as I play.

The Leaves

By: LaMont Walker

The wind blew in the leaves
But there was no sound.
Some leaves waved in the direction of the wind
While others stood still.

He felt like the leaves in the wind.
Sometimes his mouth is moving,
But the sound goes into the ears of others as silence.
At moments he'll go with the flow
To flee from all of the rigamorow.
Then at times he refuses to be moved.

Tons of leaves covered the branches,
But they were unseen.
How do we know it's a branch?
Because leaves only grow on trees.
Still how do you know something you can't see?
It has the look, shape, and moves
So it must be a branch.

He looked like a man.
He dressed like a man.
He walked like a man, a man, a man.
Just like the branch, he was covered in leaves.
So he must be a man.

Two Persons

By: LaMont Walker

As you sat across the room,

Your eyes and lips let sleep zoom.

Your head slowly bobbed

And you wouldn't let your mouth slob.

You opened your mouth and spoke

Then emotion quickly awoke.

Your hands wrote on internal tablets.

They told of a story about moral outlets.

What's on the inside of those glossy eyes?

Sometimes people don't understand your painful cries.

Love, or more realistically, lust walked out

And hurt and longing challenged for 1st in a bout.

You were worn out from blows deep,

Which during the day you now always sleep.

The Black Rose

By: LaMont Walker

A black rose was given today

As the night came to a close.

Immediately upon transferring from one hand to the next

The receiver slowly began to morph.

After the transformation

All that was left was a heartless being.

Not able to love, smile, or know joy

Because of the power of the black rose.

The black rose only affects those who love;

Those who love the giver of the black rose.

The black rose has a minimal amount of power

But the giver is the true source.

The giver knows, but ignores and takes advantage

Of the love the receiver radiates.

Even the receiver's love can't match the power of the black rose

Because real and true love knows no resistance;

Only the results of the black rose.

Internal Pieces of 'The Black Rose':

I wrote this piece to display my creative abilities. You will never find a black rose for roses in their original state are the color red. I chose to use the color black because it often associated with power and death. I chose the flower rose because it is used to symbolize love. Power, death and love are all very real experiences.

The shadow of this piece stands to speak that we have all loved someone or something that could not love us in return. True love knows no boundaries other than the ones that are set by the recipient of that love. At the point that the recipient choses to refuse the love given, it causes the giver to begin to shut down. Hence, no love, joy, or smile. There is only one remedy for one who has received a black rose, and that is true love must be given again to restore such an one.

Reminisce

By: LaMont Walker

The day is done and now I meditate

For in just a few hours I'll graduate.

This journey has been a long road

But my struggles and triumphs have yet to be told.

As a freshman living in Donnelly's stack,

Now in my own apartment I sit and look back.

Michael suckered me in,

Opportunity allowed me to sin,

God, through Jesus Christ extended grace

And LBC soared straight to 1st place.

Bingham, after church was the spot,

Where we would reflect on the word and laugh a lot.

Bishop Bootsy and mothers Mammy, Ernestine,

Dina and Ruby gave me the name Elda;

As pastor of the House of Shining Stars I always held a,

Held a space in my heart and there they gained,

But no one knew that a few years later I would be ordained.

Eddie came along singing a new song

And I laughed at myself for teaching a part that was wrong!

That was wrong of Alanda for making me listen,

But if she hadn't, I now realize all of the fun I'd be missing.

My degree in music means so much more

It will enable my cousins, brothers, and sister to walk through the same door.

They don't have to do music as I did,

But it will take them less time to walk the grid.

A huge accomplishment and yes I'm proud,

To God be the glory I'll always sing aloud!

A Time and Three Beings

By: LaMont Walker

It's that time again, Christmas;

When half of the country goes broke for man.

A toy here and there a bracelet

While people overlook the lifestyle left as a template.

Just a few days ago,

I realized this was the first time people could sleep with freedom.

As far as the planet Mars,

Somewhere locked behind bars,

My soul longs to relate.

Relate to the one whose blood I share

And review the past, but celebrate our future.

Enormous amounts of beauty

Shines on the outside of A land,

But is magnified as one takes a closer look.

Too delicate for hard impassible hands,

And not weak in mind, body, or soul.

The merry-go-round has come full circle

And now you're sick.

You got on and go what you wanted at the time

But the sadness in tone reflects the immaturity.

That was chosen over this Christian,

But This recovered and longs for lost time.

The One and You

By: LaMont Walker

The rhymes, the dimes, the nickels, and crimes

Are enough to make a mad man scream.

Not many young men are having visions

And meager portions of old men are dreaming dreams.

When will it all end?

As soon as The One called Jesus will descend.

It is all predicated upon one man, One.

At the moment that One moves, all moves.

Once One speaks, all is silent.

Yes, when One rests, all will rest.

Too much of this and too little of that

Causes deepness like that of a wine vat.

Having been labeled by many as a smooth cat,

Doesn't negate the fact that there is a crack.

The walls of strength and stability have been breached,

By the Clan of Lack resulting in insecurity.

When will it all end?

As soon as the one known as You ascend.

Much is determined and ordered by one, You.

The second You make up Your mind to wait, it all comes.

When You live and work above the status quo, all is satisfied.

Yes, once You stand for right, all will be challenged.

Dissonance

By: LaMont Walker

Dissonance: discord

Discord:Lack of agreement/harmony; dissension, conflict

A harsh combination of musical sounds

A harsh or unpleasant sound

No major 3rds, perfect 4ths, or 5ths

Just minor 2nds, tritones, and major 7ths

A call from my brother, who is angry at another,

One so close who he could suffocate or smother.

The discord in the brotherhood could,

Would, should be terminated

Causing the dissonant sound to be exterminated.

The screams, the cries, the sighs,

All indicate the lack of agreement

Between the creature and The One Who sits up high;

No harmony in the mind and a major chord of peace I can't find,

The soul is searching for some sweet expressive chimes,

The search turning up nothing but this ability to bust a rhyme,

Not even the rhyme is able to avoid dissonance

Because in between the lines are found all types of distance.

The space from one word, one line to the next

Explain how a heart felt the pain caused by an ex.

The unpleasant sound of "I don't wanna be with you"

Caused a disruption in the harmony of my picture perfect view.

I saw me with you while you clung tight to another boo

As the words spoken created a harsh feeling like that of a token.

Bought by a one dollar bill but stretched into 4 pieces;

Spent on game after game while you enjoy your Reese's.

Once the adrenaline stops, you leave, there I stay at the bottom
Until another lifts me up from Sodom.

Everybody has some dissonance,
It's just that others begin fortissimo
While some only ride the lowliness of pianissimo.
All dissonance isn't bad,
It's just those who don't understand the theory or its purpose that get mad.

Get mad, get even, or die broke trying.
To this conclusion I've unequivocally arrived;
The dissonance that sounds in my life,
I will transform, I will create the most beautiful combinations of euphemism.

Angel of Light

By: LaMont Walker

The inspiration for this rhyme
Came from within a soul giving me time
Stepping out of time and into eternity
Not knowing that your soothing voice was calming me.
Devotion, emotion, your pretty face, what a notion?
Who, I sang no shouldah, couldah, wouldahs
Because I don't serve a small fat man named buddah.

The creation, combination, that make you a unique formation
Some say corn, others say filet,
But I choose to say angel of light in this new day.
May came and may went, may we walk this way
For we don't know what gifts, blessings ahead for us lay

Don't come on too strong,
But don't be soft like charmin,
Because Valentine's day isn't for those charming.
Just enough of this and little hint of that,
Makes for the best wine pressed in this hidden vat.

I'm moving swiftly in the still of night
No, not creeping, no not sleeping, only doing what is right
I received the approval of the bishop next to the king
And I'm positioned to check the mate, so make your next move...DING!

The Sun Flower
By: LaMont Walker

Touch me, feel me, but don't play me.
Be the sun and I'll be the flower that feeds of you
And the more I feed the wider the view.
Take your time and don't rush the innocence
The innocence of the relationship between the sun and the flower
For when the two connect nothing can deny the power
The synergy of two different elements
Needing each other to help keep the world's rotation and harmony.

The sun and the light that it gives must never
Be taken for granted
Or else the flower and all of its delicacy
Could never fully blossom

Speak to the clouds and command them to move
Open your mouth to the rains and demand them to stop
Stand against the lightning and declare the radiance of the sun
Call the flower and summon the beauty within
That all who can, may be captivated by its story.

Rush

By: LaMont Walker

Rushing caused my mind to dissipate
When that happened there was a collision
For I did not take the time to think,
As I came close to the dangerous brink.
There is a song that says, "You're on the brink of a blessing..."
But rushing tricked me into making it a messing

What really happens when you rush?
You're capacity for wise judgment is diminished;
Rushing causes you to show your behind
And really lets you know how far you are behind
I'm sick of people foolishly rushing around me
Slow your role and let someone with wise counsel speak!

Rush no more, cry no more.
Rush no more, laugh some more.
Rush no more, live a little more.
Let someone who rushed to work on 9/11 speak.

Not Long

By: LaMont Walker

No one to tell but everyone would listen
To the story of a man who's not Nixon
Hearing the words as the plot unfolds
Hoping that the happily ever after is what the future holds
This poor man cried in the midst of adversity
Wondering when he would be free from the man made atrocity
Is there help? Can it be on the way?
When will the sun break the night from day?

I know that it won't be long
The choices won't always be wrong
I know that it won't be long
There's freedom within this song

When you've messed up time and time again
And it seems that the stench has hit the fan
Who do you turn to? Where do you run?
Not to a man and don't you pick up that gun
There is an answer you must see
And it comes from The One who's in eternity
The Word says come unto Me
And I'll give you life more abundantly

I know that it won't be long
The choices won't always be wrong
I know that it won't be long
There's freedom within this song

You've got to know it's not over
Until God says it's over

You're gonna come out, you're gonna win
Stay in Me and your enemies I'll defend

Not long...

Overseer Ware

By: Lamont Walker

Overseer, overseer, overseer Ware, overseer Ware

A priest, a prophet, provider, protector

The element that's needed I call the activator

He gets it started right from the jump

And when The Spirit starts flowing move over cause he'll bump.

One with an anointing to follow, teach, and lead

Causes the weak to fade and the strong to plead.

Overseer, overseer, overseer Ware, overseer Ware

Initially complex to understand

But rightly so when there's a demand

A demand from God to turn around

Away from familiar and towards fertile ground

Though you might not like him

In God's eyesight he's still a gem.

So you better watch it. Why? Yes, because he's…

Overseer, overseer, overseer Ware, overseer Ware

The Song of Solomon he sings to his wonderful love

And she replies with the proper refrain from our God above.

He asked her will you and she said I do

And a few years later here comes Kailey Morgan too!

These two special ladies have made his life brand new

He often speaks highly of them telling of what's good and true.

Overseer, overseer, overseer Ware, overseer Ware

The power of his music and preaching carries a mighty punch

And if you don't get it, he'll say you'll catch Tuesday at lunch!

Playing on the keys have made his fingers bleed

But he continued on so souls hungry for The Word could feed.

Being passed down in bib over hauls
Not knowing an anointing for the organ was about to hit and coverall!

Yes overseer, overseer, overseer Ware, overseer Ware
15 years strong and still going.
One day being the pastor of United he's already knowing.
Handling the flock, correcting those that mock,
Trying to get the deaf to open their ears to hear the knock.
The knocking of The Savior, Jesus Christ is His name
Because he's a witness if you open up your life will never be the same.
Yes he does, cause he's overseer, overseer, overseer Ware, overseer Ware.

Now that it's my chance to honor a great man
I 1st want to thank you for giving me a helping hand
You might not remember, but I do, when we spoke
In the stadium building, at the time, my life, the enemy tried to choke.
You allowed me to express the me that nobody else can see
And you gave a word from the living God, through your ability to see.
Thank you for setting a Godly standard of how to be a man
For now I know I must rise to teach the same to the young clan
For one so great there's so much to be said
And this comes from the heart, yes, this that's being read.
Be encouraged, be encouraged man of God!
Be steadfast, steadfast, unmovable, unmovable
Always abounding in the work of the Lord.
Knowing, knowing this, knowing this
That your labor is not, is not in vain!
God bless, God bless, God bless,
Overseer, overseer, overseer Ware, overseer Ware!

The Sound of Death

By: LaMont Walker

An overdue arising

Caught by surprising

Me, to find out I was late.

No, not me, not late, not again;

Then there was silence…

And the sound of death started.

I ran, I rushed, I hushed, and brushed

Only to pound the stake of tardiness further into my discombobulated conscience.

Stop! Go! Stop! Go!

There was no road for me to flow.

I made it to the destination out of breath,

Only to hear the deep piercing sound of death.

Death tried to shake me,

Tried to break me,

But I couldn't be moved

Because I had found the groove.

I was ready to unlock and unload,

All of the anger and bitterness that made me cold.

It was already forty degrees and trying to warm up

But the sound of death was so harsh, so cold, that it shattered the frozen cup.

The contents of the cup quickly fell out and responded to the sound of death…

No more sound!

No more death!

I will live forever!

Forever tardy!

I will be late again!

No more sound of death!

A Thought's Plead

By: Lamont Walker

Sitting in a room filled with minds uninhibited

The endless possibility of love and passion being unrestricted.

As two minds engage in landlords and tenants unlimited;

One mind is hoping to connect with another that has been inflicted;

Not with sickness, illness, or disease;

But with the thoughts of a one who longs to please.

How often will you think of me and my smile?

After you've hugged and left, can we still go the extra mile?

Think on these things and you're promised to have joy,

Now more of a man and no more immature thoughts of a boy.

Think of me as I think of you

And let your mind be filled with images that are new.

I am new. My laugh is new. My unforgettable smile is new.

So again and not for the last time,

Think of me as I think of you.

Awake! Awake!

By: Lamont Walker

Awake! Awake! It's time for the earth to quake!
Shake that which cannot be shaken
And take that which cannot be taken!
Awake! Awake! It's time for the earth to quake!

Comfort & Joy

By: LaMont Walker

Tis the season to be jolly

But tell me how, when the world is full of folly?

The meaning of yuletide escapes our mind

And from what is seen causes our eyes to grow blind.

Blind to the fact that the true meaning of Christmas is out of whack

And it's evident that to the manger we must turn back!

God rest ye merry gentlemen let nothing you dismay

Remember Christ our Savior was born on Christmas day

To save us all from Satan's power when we were gone astray

O tidings of comfort and joy, comfort and joy

O tidings of comfort and joy!

Joy to the world, the Lord is come

To save the rich, the meek and even the bum.

However this news was only good to some

For not everyone wants to walk to the beat of His drum.

It's a glorious sound of jubilee

For all sinners can now be reconciled to God you see!

From God our heavenly Father a blessed angel came

And unto certain shepherds brought tidings of the same

How that in Bethlehem was born the Son of God by name

O tidings of comfort and joy, comfort and joy

O tidings of comfort and joy!

Hark! The herald angels sing

While the enemy is loose releasing his sting.

The people are franticly shopping to and fro

Becoming more and more depressed don't you know!

In Macy's and Dillard's you won't find the definition,
Time to pray, is truly my intuition!

Fear not then, said the angel, let nothing you affright
This day is born a Savior of a pure virgin bright,
To free all those who trust in Him from Satan's power & might
O tidings of comfort and joy, comfort and joy
O tidings of comfort and joy!

Now to the Lord sing praises, all you within this place,
And with true love and brotherhood each other now embrace
This holy tide of Christmas doth bring redeeming grace.
O tidings of comfort and joy, comfort and joy
O tidings of comfort and joy!

*Contains lyrics of "God Rest Ye Merry Gentlemen" published 1833, author unknown.

Put The Pieces Together

By: Lamont Walker

Scattered pieces of the puzzle
Causes me to need a muzzle.
Cover my mouth to keep my thoughts in
And open my mind and you'll find yourself within.
I had to twist my personality
To make it fit the commonality.
Turn my anger around
And I connected my feelings of love to abound.
Hours spent trying to get the whole picture;
My life, your hands, you'll never have to fixture.

Birthday

By: LaMont Walker

The birthday is typically a day of celebration
One that marks the time of parturition.
That's common, however this is not.
Let's step into an unknown realm called extraordinary.

Birth: origin, beginning
Day: the period of light between one night and the next

You, being alone but not really by yourself
Causes you to do a double-take in the mirror above the shelf
Viewing the image of God's created glory
Forcing you to reflect on your life's untold story.
For at a moment was your night time
They say that things go bump in the night
Causing one to fright because there is no light;
However I say continue on;
For the darkest hour is just before day.
When you made your subtle entrance
The shine broke thru and filled the entire atmosphere.
A ray of hope and a glimpse of joy since you are near
You are the right bright that moves away from the night
So engage in festivities of the merriest kind
As it is there with robust laughter you'll find
That the night is coming again and this light will go out
But remember that your birthday is;
The beginning of light between one night and the next
So whatever isn't born today, will be born tomorrow
And in knowing that, there will never ever be sorrow.
Happy Birthday!

If I Cry

By: LaMont Walker

There is a mouth that remains sealed
While the tear ducts are quickly being filled;
Yet the eyelids refuse to open.

A heart that feels pain and void simultaneously
From external influences that have resided within.
Messages have been sent to the control center
That would signal it's time to let the water enter.
Come into the eyes and release the agony that's within.

Message after message and signal after signal
Yet the eyelids seem unresponsive.
How could this be?
Isn't there life and blood still flowing from the sea?
The sea of love, liberty, and gaiety...
That's what I'm supposed to feel because of where I am.

Where am I?
I'm in a place surrounded by people.
I'm in a place with much electricity.
I'm in a place...
Here where there are many hurt, broken, wounded, and suffering people.
So much pain and so many crying...

However, if I cry...
If I cry it will be because of the luvv I have for you
The luvv that reaches and grabs a hold of the source that sustains.
If I cry it will be because I've lost my connection.
If I cry, I will lose part of me and everyone will see the real me.

Not many will like what they see and I can't risk the verbal badgering.

Too much to hold if I cry.

All of this would happen...if I cry.

Dancing

By: LaMont Walker

The rhythm, tempo, and sounds,
Created and carried by waves in musical bounds,
Causes the feet to tap and fingers to snap.
C-walk, two-step, and even the bus stop
Are just a few new fashions since the bunny hop.
The football and the body-chop used to lead,
Then along came the body to the floor known as the centipede.

The load of books, bags, and stress
Have been lifted and the weary soul found rest.
Enough rest to rejuvenate the feet
Enabling them to skip to the beat.

No longer having to be stiff and silent,
But possessing the power to leap and vent.
A body able to express the internal pulse
That's been longing to be exhibited.

Have you yearned for anything?
Did you ever love while hurting?
Would you be willing to let go?
Let go and allow your body to flow
Rock and sway to a liberty that's never slow
Use your arms, knees, legs, and be smooth
And you'll feel the energy of this groove.

Oh My Frickin' Gorah!

By: LaMont Walker

Oh my frickin gorah!
How could I ignorah!
You wanted to be seen
After hearing the description of the beauty queen
An image appeared after being dipped in the photo room
And the Temptations lyrics scrolled,
You know, the song about being a broom...

Oh my frickin gorah!
How could I ignorah!
You were being whispered in another's ear
Who couldn't remember your image for a whole year.
Hurry! Quick! Make a dash! In a flash!
The king needs to see the queen before there's a bash,
You know, like the whole in the wall after its been mashed...

Oh my frickin gorah!
How could I ignorah!
A message sent my way and a clip of another
Pulled two worlds together without causing a smother...
The musical jargon can go on and on non-stop
But it might cause a heartbeat, or smile to not rise to the top
You know, like the sun does on a regular basis...

Oh my frickin gorah!
How could I ignorah!
I know he's looking at you, while you like me, and I love him and like you...
What a mess I would've missed
If I wouldn't have given you my number and his...

You know, like hoping that you would and wouldn't call...

Oh my frickin gorah!
How could I ignorah!
My heart!

Is There One?

By: LaMont Walker

Is there one?

Is there one who's had no fun?

Oh my gosh I wanna run!

My left and right consumed with a ton

Of one and two who's had much fun!

I try to give the benefit of doubt

At times doubt don't benefit so it turns out.

Hello! How are you? I'm fine! Me too!

Until it's found you're in the crew!

The rain came low and hit the bow

That made me want to row, row, row, and row!

There is a secret no one will tell,

But crumbs are dropped so follow the trail.

However be forewarned the more you walk

The one you seek you can't hear them talk.

How do I know? Because much have I done;

And along the way I had so much fun!

Too bad, so sad, on the flip I am glad

Because knowing what I know keeps me from being mad.

So...

Is there one who's not had the chip in the tip of the dip?

I don't know...

Pieces of Spirituality

The favorite part of this section is that these pieces are a direct connection to the passion that I have for my Lord and Savior, Christ Jesus! This section will also provide the path to Him for a more intimate relationship with Him. His luvv is incomparable and you will not be able to resist His luvv. He is the ultimate lover! He lives and I luvv Him!

"When"

By: LaMont Walker

When you try as hard as you can
To grow from a boy to a man
There are many hurts and tears
As you attempt to endure without any fears

When you strive to keep from crying
The truth of the matter is you feel like dying
You've laughed and you've smiled
But your silent hurt still cries aloud

There's a little sun that has to shine
Reaffirms everything will be just fine
Sit back and relax your clouded mind
A refreshing hope you will find
If you only you knew when

When I've wanted somebody that didn't want me
I bottled it up and threw it into the sea
When in reality I tried not to see
That the heart of the sea was inside of me

When I persevered to move on
My mind never saw a new dawn
When I had to be in the bright light
Most people couldn't even see the inner fight

There's someone who wants to bring you through
One who's strong and longs to love on you
It's the Father with wide stretched arms
Don't worry your soul He'll never harm

And He wants to ask you when

When will you stop hiding your pain from Me
I AM, you're not invisible to see
I'm always available to hear your every need
Your hungry soul I really want to feed
Today is the day your broken heart I'll mend
Remember I'm with you until the end
No more wondering
Now you know when

I'm gonna run to You
I'm gonna run to You
Today my heart You'll mend
All because I now know when

Hiyah

By: LaMont Walker

It is by grace many are saved

When Jesus died the debt was paid

His mercy never will decay

Heaven and earth shall pass away

Will you be ready when He comes?

Or when He comes will He catch you with your work undone

I gave my heart and took it back

Every time I sinned, He never slacked

His grace is sufficient believe

Accept Him and you can receive

I now can live with Him eternally

And whom the Son has set free indeed is free

Hiyah

I'm free

He reigns, oh yes Jesus reigns

He Cares for You

By: LaMont Walker

There are times when things are going fine
And you have every piece of your mind
There are times when you're feeling low
Like you have no place to go
Jesus is always there
To answer every prayer
Cast your cares on Him
For He cares for you

Cast your cares on Him
On Him you can depend
In Him you'll always win
For He cares for you

He cares, for me
I know He cares, for me

Show Me Thy Glory

LaMont Walker

This was all a part of Your plan
Gave a divine vision to a man
Saw many souls that would be free
And forever change history

He went into the tabernacle
He said Lord I beseech thee
If I've found favor in Your sight
Then show me Your glory
Show me Thy glory

Now unto thee oh great God we come
Not asking for riches, like some
But right now this is our prayer and plea
Don't let us leave without Your glory

Lord here we stand
Needing a touch from Your hand
Open our eyes so we can see
So we can see Your glory
Show me Thy glory

Show me Thy glory
We need Your glory

In the Name of Jesus Its Got to Go!!

By: Alyse Fitzpatrick

You feel pain and sadness taking it's toll
In the name of Jesus it's got to go
When suffering is putting you in a choke hold
In the name of Jesus it's got to go
There's a spirit of fear that's taken a hold
In the name of Jesus it's got to go
The lust of the world has got you in its pull
In the name of Jesus it's got to go
Depression has taken root deep down in your soul
In the name of Jesus its got to go
Jealousy has overtaken your heart and drug it down low
In the name of Jesus its got to go
Hate and raging anger has given you a low blow
In the name of Jesus its got to go
Fatigue and weariness weighted you down making you slow
In the name of Jesus its got to go
Complaining and a negative spirit always telling you no
In the name of Jesus its got to go
Hypocrisy and lying lips that are quick to flow
In the name of Jesus its got to go
Envy and the secret desire to be the star of every show
In the name of Jesus its got to go
Back biting and the constant gossip to always stay in the "know"
In the name of Jesus its got to go
When you are being unfairly treated by your foes
In the name of Jesus its got to go
Finances so low got you feeling like a hobo
In the name of Jesus its got to go
Sin in your life has you walking on death row
In the name of Jesus its got to go

Unforgiveness harbored making your heart cold as snow
In the name of Jesus its got to go
Storm and waves crashing pulling you out in the undertow
In the name of Jesus its got to go
People always hating not letting you grow
In the name of Jesus its got to go

Therefore God exalted him to the highest place
and gave him the name that is above every name,
[10]that at the name of Jesus every knee should bow,
in heaven and on earth and under the earth,
[11]and every tongue confess that Jesus Christ is Lord,
to the glory of God the Father.
Phillipians 2: 9-11

Coming for You

By: Alyse Fitzpatrick

Charged up

Fired up

But when it comes time to follow up

I feel dried up

Tied up

Don't want to empty my cup before I lift it up

Gotta get rid of all the junk

Because in your nostrils I'm smellin worse than a skunk

Thinkin and contemplating gives me an overwhelming feeling

Lord, my heart needs healing

Felt lots of pain when you chose to start revealing

Your plan and how I wasn't walking in it

And if I didn't get right, I too could be thrown into hell's pit

Lord, help me quit

For eternity at your feet is where I want to sit

Your cross is heavier than I thought I'll admit

But I'm gonna pick it up anyway

Deny myself and follow you today

I've got to break away

I'm hurting, but I know I'm okay

Keeping my eyes on you, even if I can only see you through tears

Knowing that you have a plan, you hold on to my worst fears

And every time I start to doubt

You use something or somebody to show me you've already worked it out

It makes me wanna SHOUT

The more you show me what you're all about

And Lord, thank you for everything you do for me

And I'm grateful that you keep on keeping me

And holding me

Gently taking control of me

Because on you I lean completely.

.

The Switch

By: Lamont Walker

I flipped the switch to see what would happen
Seeing thought provoking sights and hearing habitual sounds tappin'
Before the switch got clicked
Let's journey back on the tick, tock
Rotating on yesterday's clock.

Living from day to day going on my merry way
Until one like me decided to have me as an invitee
Like a respectable guest I honored the request
Not knowing that my emotions couldn't stand the test.
Tested to see if I could handle moving from up to down
From happiness to sadness, from a smile to a frown
In the beginning I held on strong
And nothing, not no one could tell me I was wrong.
I could move from church to street
And do it in the matter of a heartbeat, heartbeat, heartbeat.
Like poison ivy makes the skin itch
I itched for healing because I hadn't mastered the switch.

The moment I searched for the opposite position
I could find no help, no knob, not one physician.
Tired of hurting, tired of suffering and all the tears;
There was no aid or solution, only fears.
Fear of being trapped until eternity.
Fear of not being loved for me.
Fear of learning that I was ill terminally.
* At the end of the rope wishing I had money like the pope *

With all hope fading fast praying that the night wouldn't last.
Throat closing tight like collapsing lungs for air I fight,

154

There seems to be no more light and only blackness.

My vision is blurred due to the radiance
The more it passed through my iris
The stronger became my observance.
Seeing what I had never seen before
Caused me to feel like that of a hungry toddler asking for more
The more I saw the more I wanted to switch
Realizing self-inflicted wounds and others I had put in a ditch.
Instantly down in my soul wasn't a chill
But the warmth of The Brilliance I could feel.
Perceiving that Something new had come about
Understanding I needed someone to talk it out.
That's when I heard, "You once were a son of darkness;
Stumbling into sin exhibiting your own selfishness;
But now that you see and know what is right,
Walk as a nation & children of light."

My heart got glad and joy overflowed
My life had changed into a Spiritual mode.
If you need your vision back
Choose a battery from the rechargeable pack
These batteries aren't found at O'Reilly's or AutoZone
But are freely given away by The One Who sits on the throne.
In that realm is nothing but right
Nothing but light…that forever remains
I have been there and you are here with sight.
Therefore, I am light.
You are light.
We are light.
So stop walking as children of the night.

Worth Gathering

By: LaMont Walker

The value of something measured by its qualities is worth.

So how can I be counted as worth when it seems I have no qualities to be measured by?

And if I have no qualities, then it might become apparent that I have no value;

And if I have no value then do I fall in the category as one unworthy?

Knowing how worth is defined, I cannot fit the definition

Simply because each measuring stick is different according to my own intuition.

See one man measures this while another man measures that

Ultimately forcing me out of the house of societal normality like the cat in the hat.

And consolation from depression and suicide try to offer me green eggs and ham,

But something deep inside causes me to say I do not want them saved I am!

I do not want them by the lake because there I know awaits me that cunning snake.

I do not want them by the knife because I have not met my destiny that presents my wife.

I do not want them by the wheel, or a pill for a thrill

Because something greater is happening and I can feel.

After all that's been presented, I'm still left wondering what is my worth.

See I was looking for what could only be seen by the eyes of men

Because I concluded that whatever they gave me shined the light within;

If I sacrificed from head to heel,

From what was given, I determined that all I was worth was a meal.

If I were a professional fool or a clown better known as a jester,

From what was given, I said to myself that I shouldn't have messed her;

Because the headache given was from anger waiting to fester;

I figured that I was only worth verbal abuse.

All of this disappointment ushered me to a familiar place;

Where I found myself in a room filled with many interesting things and much space.

I took my time and looked around and I found a box with my name on it.

I figured since it had my name, then the contents must belong to me;

So I opened it up to see what I could see.

Inside of it was giving and a message that read:

"Multiple boxes for owner please keep together and call me."

Immediately I viewed the other boxes and to my surprise each one had my name on it!

After opening up every box and realizing what was inside,

I recognized I had the power and I started to speak;

Love come to me;

Forgiving I call thee;

Faithful I summon you and Joy you know what to do;

Sense of humor move and become like a phony rumor;

Giving you were first so assume your position;

Passion & compassion ya'll get tight to the right;

Warrior strength here and now and get ready for the fight.

Protector stand over me for the rest of eternity.

After calling out every content of every box,

There stood before me the form of a man that I had seen but never paid any attention;

It was God but not only God, the God that was inside of me!

He spoke and said these are the qualities that you had given

To all of the wrong places where you were driven.

I'm turning the time from midnight into My Son's light

Because your weeping over the lost qualities caused Me to exert My might!

You had them all the time, but you never knew it;

And through ever tear, ache, and pain, I brought you through it!

Just for this reason that I might tell you,

Though you were lost and scattered everywhere,

I gave of My Son whose life was able to be measured

And the quality of his works most, but not everyone treasured.

The quality of His blood couldn't tell of His origin, only that He was human.

He became lifeless because that was the value you unknowingly demanded.

I had to let His actions avail to no end,

That's why you're here my friend!

You had to call, summon, and collect all of you before going away

So that in knowing your true worth, you'll always stay.

You're worth is in Me and I AM forever;

Therefore your worth is forever so question it again never!

Welcome to your worth gathering!

Freedom

By: LaMont Walker

Have you ever been locked down?

Felt you were level to the ground;

No place to go;

The devil had you fa'sho

Couldn't see your way out

No time for doubt

Pressure weighing on you

Don't know what to do

My child I AM here...

I'll give you the power to conquer your fears

I know that you wanna be free

Wanna be free...free me to be more like Thee

Now where do I begin

To walk in this freedom again?

Been bound so long...

I didn't know right from wrong.

Can I get up?

Will He fill my cup?

How long will this last?

Won't you free me from my past?

My child I AM here...

I'll give you the power to conquer your fears

I know that you wanna be free

Wanna be free...free me to be more like Thee

Free me

Wanna walk in liberty

It's only by Your blood
That I can be redeemed from the flood

The flood of my emotion
The flood of all the commotion
Waging a war within me
Trying to keep me from my liberty
Free me

I'm coming just for you
I will bring you through
I AM the chain breaker
I will break the chains
Freedom…

Time to shout some Praise

By: Alyse Fitzpatrick

The tentacles of sin

They are strangling me from within

They took hold because I gave in

But I can't let it win

Gotta get back up again

A righteous man may fall but seven times he gets back up

Throws out the filth then lifts up his empty cup

It says it in Proverbs 24, get ya word, look it up

says that if I'm sleepin I'll be poor…time to Wake UP!

What you may not know is satan is a provider too

He'll give you anything and everything to try to destroy you

He'll kick you while you're down turn you all black and blue

Most of us are falling for his tricks, we haven't got a clue

Time to shout some praise, let's fight this battle

Sound the trumpet, shake that tambourine like a baby shakes its rattle

Get to stompin so hard we're sounding like a herd of cattle

Open up your mouth like when you were little and you would tattle

These weapons are mighty through God to the pulling down of strongholds

I know it's true, I read it in the word, the victory has already been foretold

It's time to get bold because Gods power we do hold

Don't just listen to what I'm saying and let your heart stay cold

It's not God's desire that any man should eternally die

But you gotta commit, He doesn't want another I'll try

Are you gonna trust that He knows best or keep asking why

Will you give up on God if you ask again and get no reply

Or will you pick up your cross and yourself you'll deny

Its not gonna be easy, I'm not gonna lie

Time to shout some praise, let's fight this battle

Sound the trumpet, shake that tambourine like a baby shakes its rattle

Get to stompin so hard we're sounding like a herd of cattle

Open up your mouth like when you were little and you would tattle

You may wonder why I've just got to praise

Maybe because of the love He gives that always stays

And also because He's shown me grace in so many ways

My God walks with me and gives me comfort on the hardest of days

When I'm feeling low my head he does raise

When I'm at a loss for words gives me phrase by phrase

Every debt I ever had and will have he pays

Anytime I feel lost he leads me out of the maze

He gives me peace and makes my mind strong and not crazed

All the power in hell won't cause my God to be phased

So I come into his courts with praise

I surrender all with my hands upraised

I exalt the ancient of days

I'll walk in His ways

Hold me tight Lord that I'll never stray

Don't be far away

That's all I've got to say

Hear me as I pray Emotions should always follow, never lead

Who, But Oh Who

By: LaMont Walker

Before the world was framed
It was already known that I would be maimed;
I am imperfect, defective, and made impair
My all is at a lost and left in despair
But written is counted the numbers of my hair;
Each breath I take causes me to lose air
Who, but oh who can again make me fair?

Time and time and time again
I find myself being a wretched man;
The things that I would do
Never seem to come to
And the things I shouldn't do
I find myself constantly following through.
Who, but oh who can break me through?

My life is in need of direction
And certainly wanted is another's protection
Because the path I walk was my selection;
Crooked and wide is the trail all the day
When straight and narrow should be the only way;
The Word is to be a lamp unto my feet
Who, but oh who, can show me the right street?

There is therefore now no condemnation
To them that walk after Me is no frustration;
You follow while I lead with no hesitation
And from the truth of it all will be no deviation.
I Am The Promise of The Promised and The Best nonetheless,
Trying to guide all away from the worldly mess.

Who, but oh who will receive Me and be blessed?

I Am He Who was and is and is to come,
Saving the rich, sophisticated, & even the bum.
The assignment was given & I completed it when I reversed the curse
And I sent out many to be lambs among wolves without a purse.
I Am The Promise of The Promised and The Knight at the right,
Praying through all who choose to walk in The Light.
Who, but oh will be ready when I come as a thief in the night?

In the beginning was The Word and The Word was with Me.
I became The Word for the whole wide world to see;
Bringing sight to the blind who thought they were fine
And daily perfecting those that I consider to be Mines.
I AM THAT I AM and thou shall have no other gods before Me,
Man-made graven images & the likeness thereof awakens jealousy in Me.
Who, but oh who, will bow down and worship Me?

Internal Pieces of 'Who, But oh Who':

One of my desires for this book is that it will save someone's life. One of the ways for this to happen was to identify with some of the commonalities of this life. I chose the point of introspection and while there I was able to determine what everyone has in common: sin, death, and the need for a savior. I have a hook of imperfection in me just like everyone else. I have done wrong just like everyone else. I need help just like everyone else. I begin this piece as a man representing man, but flip the piece to be a mouthpiece for the answer to the questions of man.

The only way to be saved from this destruction is the way of Jesus Christ, Who said, "I am the way, the truth, and the life." (St. John 14:6 KJV) I hope through this piece written, you are able to identify with me and come to the same conclusion that Jesus is the way to the best life you will ever experience!

The Master Plan

By: LaMont Walker

My precious people still bound by sin
Yet they have a yearning for freedom deep within.
The darkness in their world clouds their opinion
Making them blind to the fact that I've given them dominion.
Over and over and over again they slip and fall
Not knowing they're still shackled to the chain and ball.
What must I do? Something can be done…

It was no accident but this was meant to be
For before the foundations of the world,
You saw much further than I could see.
One came to die that all might live
And Your only begotten Son was who You had to give.
The question was raised in the heavens above,
"Who will go to show My love?"
For a time and space there was silence in that place;
Until one spoke and declared I will become the ultimate sacrifice.

You will be lied on….I still will go.
You will be spit on….I still will go.
You will be kicked….I still will go.
You will be beaten….I still will go.
You will be stretched, hung, & left for dead…but I still will go.
For that I will give you a name above all names…And I still will go.

Being born of a virgin girl named Mary
He completed His task and did not tarry.
From water to wine, from a man to the swine,
All things were done as the Master said they would be,
But not many counted on what they couldn't see!

Resurrection power entered the earth & raised Him who once was dead
And now He feeds those who are willing to be fed!
Feast on eternal life that's found only in Him
The One and Only True Royal Diadem.
His power and Word never diminish
And you and I never have to die because He said "It is finished."
The end is coming and don't wait too late,
For His second return is soon and we don't know the date!

The Steps to Being Saved

Step 1: Realizing God's Love for You

- "For God so loved the world that He gave His only begotten Son, that whosoever believes in Him shall not perish, but have everlasting life." – St. John 3:16

Step 2: Realizing You're Not The Only One Needing Salvation

- "For all have sinned, and come short of the glory of God" – Romans 3:23

Step 3: Realizing Christ Died For You

- "But God commended His love toward us, in that, while we were yet sinners, Christ died for us." – Romans 5:8

Step 4: Realizing God's Gift to You

- "For the wages of sin is death, but the gift of God is eternal life through Jesus Christ our Lord."- Romans 6:23

Step 5: Realizing That It Takes Your Faith & Not Works

- "For by grace are you saved through faith; and that not of yourselves: it is the gift of God: Not of works, lest any man should boast." – Ephesians 2:8-9

Step 6: Realizing The Way to Get Saved

- "That if thou shall confess with they mouth the Lord Jesus, and shall believe in your heart that God hath raised Him from the dead, thou shall be saved. For with the heart man believeth unto righteousness; and with the mouth confession is made unto salvation." – Romans 10:9-10

If you have followed the path, the final step to salvation is to pray the sinners prayer. If you are ready, prayer the following out loud:

Father in heaven, I (state your name) thank You for sending Your son Jesus to die for me and to pay for my sins. I believe You raised Him from the dead. Now, Jesus, I ask You to come into my heart and to cleanse me of my sins, to be my Lord and to make heaven my home. I now confess with my mouth that You, Jesus, are my Lord. Thank you, Father, that I am now saved! I have eternal life with You! In Jesus' name, I pray. Amen.

Congratulations! You are now saved and the angels in heaven are rejoicing over you! If you have just taken the steps to salvation, please contact us at:

His Word His Way

P. O. Box 10043

Columbia, MO 65205

(573) 529-1221 – Office

Overseerwalker@gmail.com

We would like to rejoice with and celebrate you! If you have not taken the steps, we pray that you have received something that will make a positive difference in your life! Jesus is the way and we know not, when He is to return, but He is coming back! Don't wait too late!

Other books by CECO Publishing

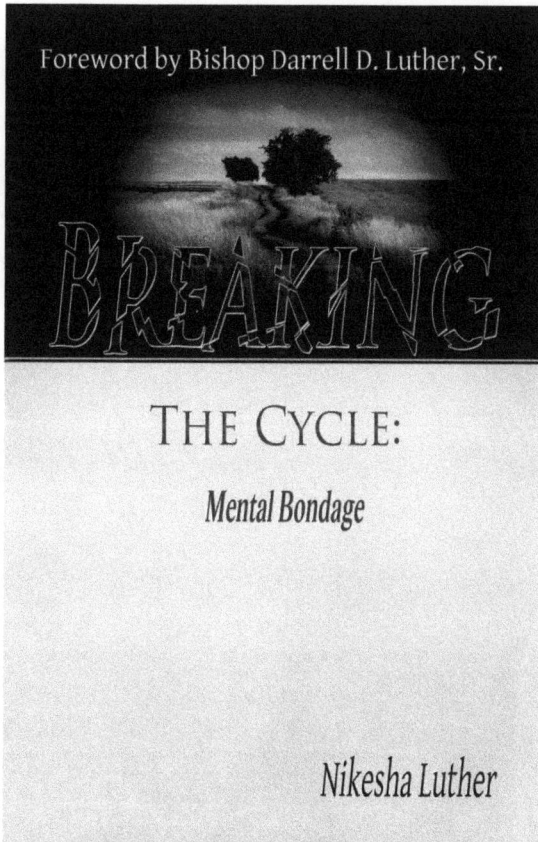

Foreword by Bishop Darrell D. Luther, Sr.

BREAKING

THE CYCLE:

Mental Bondage

Nikesha Luther

In Breaking the Cycle: Mental Bondage Pastor Nikesha Luther teaches the important role vision plays in staying free of mental bondage and living the life of purpose God has for you.

To purchase please visit: www.cecofellowship.org/Store.html

Other books by CECO Publishing

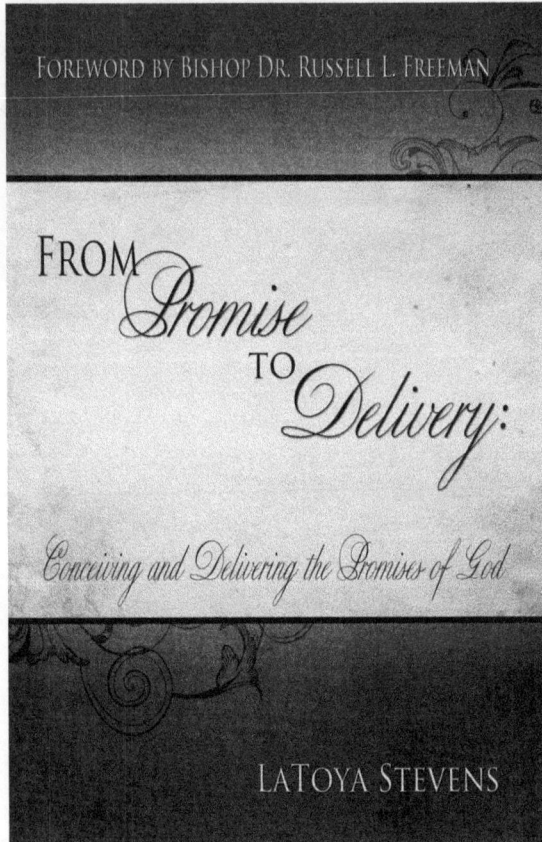

In *From Promise to Delivery*, Elder LaToya Stevens discusses how as believers, we often wonder why we don't see the promises God has made to us come to pass. This book will help the reader identify what is stopping them from conceiving, carrying, and delivering the promises of God.

To purchase go to: www.cecofellowship.org/Store.html

www.ingramcontent.com/pod-product-compliance
Lightning Source LLC
Chambersburg PA
CBHW030934090426
42737CB00007B/424